OVERRIDING THE MARKS OF THE BEAST

PRAYERS

DR. Y. BUR

Available Titles

ASITPLEASESGOD.COM

OVERRIDING THE MARKS OF THE BEAST PRAYERS

A Pathway To Renewal

Copyright © 2026 by R.O.A.R. Publishing Group. All rights reserved.

Visit www.DrYBur.com or www.AsItPleasesGod.com for more information. No part of this publication may be reproduced, stored in a retrieval system, or transmitted in any way by any means, electronic, mechanical, photocopy, recording, or otherwise, without the prior permission of the author, except as provided by USA copyright law. All rights reserved.

R.O.A.R. Publishing Group
581 N. Park Ave. Ste. #725
Apopka, FL 32704
ROAR-58-2316
762-758-2316
www.RoarPublishingGroup.com

AIPG Donation Link

Scan to Pay

Published in the United States of America
ISBN: 979-8-9990619-8-0
$24.88

ASITPLEASESGOD.COM

Send AS IT PLEASES GOD

Book Series **and** *Workbook* **Testimonies, Donations, or Orders to**

Dr. Y. Bur
R.O.A.R. Publishing Group
581 N. Park Ave. Ste. #725
Apopka, FL 32704
ROAR-58-2316
762-758-2316

Dr.YBur@gmail.com

Visit Us At:
AsItPleasesGodMovement
AsItPleasesGod

DrYBur.com
AsItPleasesGod.com

Please Donate

Please DONATE to this *Missionable Movement of God* as a GIVE-BACK to the Kingdom. Thanks for your support. Many Blessings.

AIPG Donation Link

Scan to Pay

Table of Contents

Prayerful Introduction 15
Prayer Override 1 17
    The Mark of Aloofness 17
Prayer Override 2 19
    The Mark of Abandonment 19
Prayer Override 3 21
    The Mark of Anger 21
Prayer Override 4 23
    The Mark of Avoidance 23
Prayer Override 5 25
    The Mark of Baiting 25
Prayer Override 6 27
    The Mark of Begging 27
Prayer Override 7 29
    The Mark of Blindness 29
Prayer Override 8 31
    The Mark of Brokenness 31
Prayer Override 9 33
    The Mark of Busyness 33
Prayer Override 10 35
    The Mark of Collapse 35
Prayer Override 11 37
    The Mark of Colorism 37
Prayer Override 12 39
    The Mark of Comparison 39
Prayer Override 13 41
    The Mark of Competitiveness 41

Prayer Override 14 43
    The Mark of Compromise 43

Prayer Override 15 47
    The Mark of Confusion 47

Prayer Override 16 49
    The Mark of Control 49

Prayer Override 17 51
    The Mark of Coveting 51

Prayer Override 18 53
    The Mark of Deafness 53

Prayer Override 19 55
    The Mark of Delusion 55

Prayer Override 20 57
    The Mark of Denial 57

Prayer Override 21 59
    The Mark of Disappointment 59

Prayer Override 22 61
    The Mark of Disobedience 61

Prayer Override 23 63
    The Mark of Disrespectfulness 63

Prayer Override 24 65
    The Mark of Dissatisfaction 65

Prayer Override 25 67
    The Mark of Distrust 67

Prayer Override 26 69
    The Mark of Division 69

Prayer Override 27 71
    The Mark of Dominance 71

Prayer Override 28 73
    The Mark of Doubt 73

Prayer Override 29 75
   The Mark of Dullness..75
Prayer Override 30 77
   The Mark of Envy and Jealousy 77
Prayer Override 31 79
   The Mark of Favoritism...79
Prayer Override 32 81
   The Mark of Fear 81
Prayer Override 33 83
   The Mark of Frailty 83
Prayer Override 34 85
   The Mark of Fixing People..85
Prayer Override 35 87
   The Mark of Gossip...87
Prayer Override 36 89
   The Mark of Greed..89
Prayer Override 37 91
   The Mark of Grouping (Stereotyping) 91
Prayer Override 38 93
   The Mark of Hatefulness 93
Prayer Override 39 95
   The Mark of Hiding...95
Prayer Override 40 97
   The Mark of Idolatry 97
Prayer Override 41 99
   The Mark of Impatience 99
Prayer Override 42 101
   The Mark of Impulsion...101
Prayer Override 43 103
   The Mark of Individuality 103

Prayer Override 44 105
    The Mark of Insaneness 105

Prayer Override 45 107
    The Mark of Insecurity 107

Prayer Override 46 109
    The Mark of Insulting Others 109

Prayer Override 47...111
    The Mark of Interruptions 111

Prayer Override 48 113
    The Mark of Judgment 113

Prayer Override 49 115
    The Mark of Lies.. 115

Prayer Override 50 117
    The Mark of Low Self-Esteem 117

Prayer Override 51 119
    The Mark of Lukewarmness 119

Prayer Override 52 121
    The Mark of Lust 121

Prayer Override 53..123
    The Mark of Mind Games 123

Prayer Override 54 125
    The Mark of Mind Reading 125

Prayer Override 55..127
    The Mark of Miscommunication 127

Prayer Override 56... 129
    The Mark of Misguidance 129

Prayer Override 57..131
    The Mark of Muteness 131

Prayer Override 58...133
    The Mark of Neediness 133

Prayer Override **59** 135
   The Mark of Neglect 135

Prayer Override **60** 137
   The Mark of Overreacting 137

Prayer Override **61** 139
   The Mark of Paranoia 139

Prayer Override **62** 141
   The Mark of Perfection 141

Prayer Override **63** 143
   The Mark of Perversion 143

Prayer Override **64** 145
   The Mark of Placement 145

Prayer Override **65** 147
   The Mark of Player Hating 147

Prayer Override **66** 149
   The Mark of Playing God 149

Prayer Override **67** 151
   The Mark of Poverty 151

Prayer Override **68** 153
   The Mark of Pretense 153

Prayer Override **69** 155
   The Mark of Pride 155

Prayer Override **70** 157
   The Mark of Ramifications 157

Prayer Override **71** 159
   The Mark of Recklessness 159

Prayer Override **72** 161
   The Mark of Regret 161

Prayer Override **73** 163
   The Mark of Rejection 163

Prayer Override 74 165
    The Mark of Resentment 165
Prayer Override 75 167
    The Mark of Rotten Fruit 167
Prayer Override 76 169
    The Mark of Self-Gratification 169
Prayer Override 77 171
    The Mark of Soul Ties 171
Prayer Override 78 173
    The Mark of Stunted Growth 173
Prayer Override 79 175
    The Mark of Struggling Sabotage 175
Prayer Override 80 177
    The Mark of the Lone Ranger Syndrome 177
Prayer Override 81 179
    The Mark of the Love of Money Maze 179
Prayer Override 82 181
    The Mark of Thievery 181
Prayer Override 83 183
    The Mark of Thwarted Perceptions 183
Prayer Override 84 185
    The Mark of Toxicity 185
Prayer Override 85 187
    The Mark of Triangulation 187
Prayer Override 86 189
    The Mark of Unfaithfulness 189
Prayer Override 87 191
    The Mark of Unforgiveness 191
Prayer Override 88 193
    The Mark of Ungratefulness 193

Prayer Override 89 195
    The Mark of Unkindness 195
Prayer Override 90 197
    The Mark of Unpreparedness 197
Prayer Override 91 199
    The Mark of Unrepentance 199
Prayer Override 92 201
    The Mark of Unrestraint 201
Prayer Override 93 203
    The Mark of Unsafety 203
Prayer Override 94 205
    The Mark of Urgency 205
Prayer Override 95 207
    The Mark of Victimization 207
Prayer Override 96 209
    The Mark of Weakness 209
Prayer Override 97 211
    The Mark of Wickedness 211
Prayer Override 98 213
    The Mark of Worthlessness 213
Prayer Override 99 215
    The Mark of the X-Factor 215
Prayer Override 100 217
    The Mark of Yoking 217
Prayer Override 101 219
    The Mark of Zombieism 219

INTRODUCTION

The Mark of the Beast has stirred fear, curiosity, aloofness, or deep Spiritual Reflection from the Ancient of Days until this very moment. The MARK represents more than a physical symbol; it signifies allegiance, identity, and the Spiritual Forces that shape our destinies, be it known or unknown. In a world increasingly influenced by systems that challenge our faith and moral convictions, we as Believers of the Most High God are called to stand firm in Divine Truth and Authority, *As It Pleases God*.

Overriding the Marks of the Beast Prayers is a Spiritual Guide designed to help Believers, like yourself, reclaim your Divine Identity and Authority through these spoken prayers. All of which focuses on breaking Spiritual Yokes and Ties, rejecting false marks, and reaffirming our Divine Alignment with the MARK of God's Divine Covenant. Through these faith-filled declarations and scriptural insights, this collection empowers Believers, once again, like yourself, to overcome deception, fear, doubt, and Spiritual Bondage.

The Power of Prayer is the Spiritual Weapon of Spiritual Warfare, requiring every Believer to RISE in discernment, purity, and character with an unwavering devotion to God, our Heavenly Father. More importantly, we must operate in DIVINE TRUTH, *As It Pleases Him*, to override the marks of darkness with LIGHT.

In *Overriding the Marks of the Beast Prayers*, as Dr. Y. Bur, The WHY Doctor, I present a powerful Spiritual Resource for those seeking liberation from fear, oppression, and Spiritual Bondage. Rooted in deep scriptural insight and compassionate understanding, these prayers are more than routine narrations of Spiritual Warfare. They are for Psychological Warfare, serving as living Spiritual Apparatuses of transformation for the psyche of mankind according to our DNA in Earthen Vessels.

The concept of the Marks of the Beast has generated anxiety and confusion within our communities of faith. Through this collection, I invite readers to confront these fears, not by retreating into superstition or conditioned fallacies, but by stepping forward into active engagement with Divine Truth, *As It Pleases God*. Each prayer is carefully crafted to dismantle the hold of negative patterns and to affirm the Divine Sovereignty of our Spirit.

What sets this book apart is the emphasis on free-willed empowerment. As The WHY Doctor, these prayers do not merely address the symptoms of our Spiritual Struggles only; they reach for the SEEDS and ROOTS of them. At the same time, guiding you through confession, renunciation, affirmation, and consecration. The process is holistic, encouraging not just a change in words, but a transformation of our heart and mind postures, *As It Pleases God*. As you immerse yourself in these prayers, you are invited to experience release from inherited burdens and to claim a renewed identity anchored in faith, love, and hope in Christ Jesus.

Overriding the Marks of the Beast Prayers is not just a book of supplications only. Instead, it is a Spiritual Manual with the Divine Language that MOVES the Heart of God, especially when reclaiming Spiritual Autonomy and resisting the forces that seek to define or diminish the human psyche.

The Divine Wisdom and Compassion from the Heavenly of Heavens shines throughout, offering practical guidance and profound encouragement for those needing a little help or an extra push. For anyone longing to break free from cycles of fear and limitation, *Overriding the Marks of the Beast* Book Collection stands as a beacon of hope, lighting the way toward Spiritual Renewal and lasting FREEDOM.

www.DrYBur.com

PRAYER OVERRIDE 1

The Mark of Aloofness

Heavenly Father, as I endeavor to live my best life amidst the demands and distractions of this world, I confess that the silent *Mark of Aloofness* has quietly crept into my heart. I acknowledge that it has eroded my authentic faith and replaced it with false illusions, obscuring Your truth with the haze of my daily struggles, challenges, and tests. Too often, I have attempted to navigate life in my own strength, unaware that the enemy has subtly veiled my eyes and dulled my Spiritual Sensitivity.

I remember that this is not a new tactic, for the adversary has been weaving deception since the Garden of Eden. Yet, I take responsibility for discerning and reversing these schemes. Grant me the wisdom to recognize the Spirit of Aloofness for what it is, refusing to downplay, camouflage, or ignore its intent to draw me away from You.

Spirit to Spirit, I humble myself before You, acknowledging that the enemy cannot overtake my mind unless I first disconnect myself from Your presence. I ask for the courage to self-correct, the humility to seek Your face, and the perseverance to guard my heart against indifference and detachment.

Lord, forgive me for the times I have taken shortcuts in my walk with You or detached myself from the process of Spiritual Growth. Empower me to labor faithfully in the vineyard of my soul, cultivating the ground You have entrusted to me. May I resist the temptation to seek idolatry, religiosity, instant gratification, and idleness, and instead pursue a life that PLEASES You with my Mind, Body, Soul, and Spirit.

Remind me that the work of Spiritual Tilling cannot be outsourced and that I must take up the call to grow, repent, and renew my commitment to You. Protect me from the Spiritual Penalties of complacency and disobedience, and give me discernment to recognize when I am being led astray.

Lord, expose the quiet influence of the Spirit of Aloofness in my life. Restore my sensitivity to Your Holy Spirit and remind me daily of the power of the Blood of Jesus as my atonement. Where I feel undervalued, misused, misunderstood, unmotivated, or unimpressed, let me see these as signals to realign myself with Your Divine Will.

I surrender my Spiritual Posture to You, asking that You would sharpen my mind and soften my heart. Strengthen my resolve to stay connected to You, to myself, and to others in true authenticity. Let Your light dispel every shadow of complacency and self-sufficiency. May I rise above every false mark and claim the freedom, renewal, and intimacy that is found only in Your presence. In Jesus' Name I pray, Amen.

PRAYER OVERRIDE 2

The Mark of Abandonment

Holy God, my Heavenly Father, in this world where connection is promised at every turn, I confess that I often feel utterly alone. I am surrounded by endless ways to reach others, yet something deep within me aches with the weight of isolation. I carry wounds from those who claimed they would stand by me, only to leave when I needed them most. I have stumbled and made mistakes, and now I try to pick up the pieces while feeling mentally and emotionally fragmented, unable to speak a word of it to anyone.

I come before You with a bleeding heart, feeling as though even reaching out to You is not bringing the comfort I long for. The words spoken in counseling sessions ring hollow. Sometimes I am left waiting on Your Divine Intervention, but the loneliness presses down in secret, growing heavier and more shameful each day. I feel *The Mark of Abandonment*, whether real or imagined, etched deep into my soul, and it challenges me to my very core.

Why do You allow me, as a Believer, to be tested in this area? I know Your Word teaches that this is the very place where many give up, turn around, compromise, or cling to things that cannot save them. In this wilderness, You call me to abandon my false sense of self-reliance, the comforts of this world, the traits and beliefs that do not PLEASE You. You invite me to let go of what I have trusted so that I can trust You completely.

I admit that the echoes of abandonment in my past, present, and future call my name loudly. I have felt the sting of being left by loved ones. I have watched their absence shake the very fabric of my being. The mark left behind is more than a scar; it is a TESTIMONY in the making if I dare to reverse engineer my pain, *As It Pleases You.*

I acknowledge that *The Mark of Abandonment* runs deep, surfacing in moments of weakness, triggering me to act out or dissociate, just as Your Word warns. I confess that sometimes I black out, trying to escape the pain. I remember Psalm 55:22. You ask me to cast my cares on You and promise to sustain me. I remember Colossians 3:2. You call me to set my mind on things above. I remember Isaiah 40:29. You give power to the weak and increase strength to those with no might.

Still, I struggle. I want You to instantly fill me with strength, but You have given me free will. The strength is inside me, but I must choose to connect and wait. You remind me in Joshua 1:9 to be strong and courageous, that You are with me wherever I go. You remind me of Isaiah 40:31 that those who wait on You will renew their strength. You teach me to connect, wait, and prepare, so I do not fall into the enemy's trap.

In the waiting, help me to prepare my heart. Teach me patience, as James 5:7-8 says, so I do not abandon my purpose or my calling. Remind me that my longing for connection is not weakness, but a reflection of how You made me. Help me face the pain I have buried, so it cannot control me any longer. Lord, when I feel abandoned, even by You, remind me that it is in these moments You are asking me to come closer, to ask the hard questions, and to seek answers that only Your Spirit can provide. Help me to see *The Mark of Abandonment* not as a curse, but as a catalyst for deeper healing, for realignment with Your Divine Purpose, and for a TESTIMONY that will one day encourage others.

Give me the courage, wisdom, and grace to stay in this process, even when it hurts. Help me to guard my heart, to reach out for real connection, and to trust that Your Spirit is working in me, even when I cannot sense it. Let me not be defined by abandonment, but by Your relentless love and the resilience You are building within me.

I surrender my wounds to You, and ask for Your Spirit to heal me from the inside out. Lead me from the shadows into Your light, and let my testimony be one of overcoming, *As It Pleases You.* In Jesus' Name I pray, Amen.

PRAYER OVERRIDE 3

The Mark of Anger

Gracious Heavenly Father, I come before You, humbled by the awareness of my own frailty and the reality of the anger within my heart. I confess that anger, at times, has shaped my words, thoughts, actions, reactions, or decisions, and even the course of my relationships. Sometimes I have allowed it to fester in secret, becoming both a shield and a sword, hurting others, and wounding myself. I acknowledge that nothing is hidden from Your sight. I stand exposed before You, longing for Your healing and transformation.

Lord, I thank You for the precious gift of Your Spirit, who brings conviction, wisdom, and comfort. I ask for Your Spirit to move powerfully within me, shining Divine Light on the roots of my anger. Show me the wounds, disappointments, and fears that have taken up residence in my soul. Teach me to recognize the difference between righteous indignation and destructive rage. Guard my heart against bitterness and resentment, and help me to surrender every feeling that does not please You.

Father, I pray for discernment to recognize my triggers. The moments, words, and memories that ignite the flames of anger in my life. Let me not be ruled by these emotions, but rather led by the Spirit of Self-Control and Peace. Fill me with the courage to pause, reflect, and seek Your Divine Wisdom before I speak or act. When I am tempted to justify my anger or lash out, remind me of the example of Jesus, who, though wronged and misunderstood, responded with love, mercy, kindness, and forgiveness.

In the moments when anger feels overwhelming, remind me of Your promise in 1 Corinthians 10:13, that You will not allow me to be tempted beyond what I can bear, and that You always provide a way of escape. Strengthen me to take that way out, even when it requires humility and sacrifice. Let Your Spirit empower me to transform anger from a force of destruction into a catalyst for healing, reconciliation, and growth, in my own life and in the lives of those around me.

Lord, I confess the times I have held onto grudges or sought revenge, rather than trusting in Your justice and grace. Forgive me for every harsh word, every bitter thought, and every unkind action or reaction. Cleanse my heart, renew my mind, and restore in me the Spirit of Righteousness. Help me to repent sincerely, to ask forgiveness where I have wronged others, and to forgive those who have wounded me. Release me from the bondage of anger, and let me walk in the freedom and peace of Your presence.

Father, I ask that You would help me to walk in the Spirit of Excellence, striving for self-control, humility, and wisdom in every circumstance. May I be quick to listen, slow to speak, and slow to anger, reflecting Your love to everyone I encounter. Let Your Spirit transform my anger into empathy where there is pain, into courage where there is injustice, and into perseverance where there are trials.

I pray for those around me who struggle with anger, that You would grant them the same grace and healing. Let our homes, our families, and our communities become places of understanding, forgiveness, and reconciliation. May we bear witness to Your transforming power, shining as lights in a world often darkened by conflict and division.

Lord, I thank You for the security I have in Your name. As Your Word says, the name of the Lord is a strong tower; the righteous run to it and are safe. I choose to run to You, to abide in Your presence, and to rely on Your strength. Help me to use my emotions for good, in ways that honor You and bring about Divine Illumination.

Thank You for Your patience, Your mercy, and Your steadfast love. Thank You for never giving up on me, even when I struggle with the same battles time and time again. I surrender *The Mark of Anger* to You, trusting that You are able to redeem even my darkest emotions for Your greater purpose.

Shape me into a vessel of Your peace and love, that I may glorify You in all things. In Jesus' Name I pray, Amen.

PRAYER OVERRIDE 4

The Mark of Avoidance

Heavenly Father, I come before You in awe of Your Divine Wisdom and mercy, deeply aware of my need for You in every hidden corner of my soul. Your Word declares that nothing is concealed from Your sight, and so I bring to You *The Mark of Avoidance* that has subtly woven itself into my heart and mind. Lord, I confess that too often I shrink back from confrontation, sidestep uncomfortable truths, and evade the call to courage that You have placed within me. I acknowledge that what sometimes feels like protection is, in truth, a hindrance that keeps me from the fullness of Your purpose.

Father, I recognize that the enemy is cunning, exploiting my instincts to avoid rather than to engage. I see how he tempts me into a cycle of inaction, laziness, and denial as he whispers that the safe path is the silent one, the comfortable one, the one where I do not have to face myself or others when it is not true in Your Divine Eye. Yet, I know You have not given me a Spirit of Fear, but of power, love, and a sound mind. Lord, awaken me to the tactics employed against me. Give me the discernment to recognize when avoidance is robbing me of my growth and authenticity.

Holy Spirit, I invite You to search the depths of my being. Shine Your light into every shadowed place where avoidance has taken root. Transform what once felt like a safe refuge into fertile ground for resilience and maturity. Teach me to see discomfort as an invitation to lean on Your strength, and to be honest, humble, and accountable in all that I do, say, become, and encounter. Let the cycle of avoidance be broken by Your truth, replaced by a willingness to face challenges with grace and courage.

Lord, You are the God who brings beauty from brokenness. You remind me that all who pass through this Earthly Realm bear marks, cracks, tears, and scars; visible and invisible, tangible and Spiritual. These are not signs of failure, but of arrival and struggle, evidence of my shared humanity and my connection to You. Even the process of birth, with its breaking and cutting, is a Divine reminder that pain and joy often coexist, and that the journey into newness requires courage, surrender, and faith.

I thank You that Jesus Himself did not bypass this Spiritual Principle. He embraced the process of being born into this world, upholding the Divine Order and Duality established by Your Divine Hand. Likewise, I yield to Your pruning process, and to the cutting away of everything that restrains or stunts my Spiritual Growth. Break every barrier of avoidance within me. Let Your refining work transform my resistance into readiness, my hesitance into hope, and my fear into faith.

Father, as I seek to override the marks of the enemy in my life, let me become a catalyst for positive, transformative greatness. Not only in myself, but in my relationships, my lessons, my experiences, and every test I face. Keep me humble, always mindful that every victory is by Your might, not my own. Let me be accountable to Your Divine Calling, to those around me, and to the Spiritual Mission and Blueprint You have set before me.

Show me, Lord, the people and situations where I need to exercise caution and pump the brakes, while discerning with wisdom and love. But never let me retreat into avoidance out of fear. Instead, let me move forward, *As It Pleases You*, confident that Your Spirit will guide, protect, and empower me for every confrontation, every truth, and every opportunity for growth. In Jesus' Name I pray, Amen.

www.DrYBur.com

PRAYER OVERRIDE 5

The Mark of Baiting

Gracious and Sovereign Father, I come before You with humility and awe, acknowledging Your Supreme Wisdom and unwavering understanding. In the maze of my emotional experiences, I confess that I have often encountered *The Mark of Baiting*. The subtle and cunning tactic employed by the enemy to lure me into places and pursuits that promise benefit, yet ultimately steal my focus and diminish my true calling in You.

Lord, I admit how easily fleeting rewards and false securities can entice my heart. I recognize how the enemy seeks to create a twist of idolatry within me, causing me to idolize the approval of others, material gain, or temporary thrills. When I play small, or beneath those who seem to possess "bigger fish," I am reminded that the snare is not always obvious. The enemy rarely presents himself as a beast but comes slyly, just as he did in the Garden, using smooth words and calculated moves to trap my mind and ensnare my Spirit.

Heavenly Father, I ask You to expose every scheme designed to prey on my vulnerabilities. Illuminate the shadowed corners where I am most susceptible to distraction and manipulation. Help me discern when my instincts are being nudged away from Your Divine Purpose, and empower me by Your Spirit to resist the temptations that seek to derail my Divine Destiny.

I confess that, at times, my senses have failed me. I have allowed my biological and neurological limits to justify impulsive choices, moving faster than wisdom would allow. I have fallen prey to the lure of quick decisions, only to regret them when the adrenaline fades and clarity returns. Yet, Your Word instructs me to be swift to hear, slow to speak, and slow to wrath. By Your Divine Grace, teach me to pause, to listen, and to wait for Your counsel before I act.

Lord, I acknowledge that my mind can be deceived, my thoughts can jump the track, and my beliefs can be swayed when I am distracted or unaware. I ask You to sharpen my Spiritual Antennas so that I may operate, *As It Pleases You*. Let me not be caught off guard by the enemy's sleight of hand. Heighten my awareness and discernment so that my responses are guided by the Spirit, not by impulse or fear.

Father, help me to distinguish the difference between positive and negative bait. Grant me the wisdom to recognize encouragement, preparation, support, and nourishment as GIFTS from You. Let me embrace that which feeds my Spirit and draws me closer to Your truth. At the same time, reveal and uproot any discouragement, disappointment, discredit, or depletion that seeks to entangle me in cycles of negativity or stagnation.

Equip me, Lord, with a renewed sense of purpose and authentic engagement. Strengthen my resolve to confront the feelings and temptations that arise with *The Mark of Baiting*. Help me to ask the honest questions, to seek the ultimate why, and to respond not with avoidance or denial, but with courage and clarity. Let me always be guided by Your Spirit, never losing sight of the light You have placed within me.

May I seek the light, share the light, and be the light in every circumstance, *As It Pleases You*. Let nothing and no one, not even *The Mark of Baiting* or *The Mark of Begging*, hold me back from walking in the fullness of Your Divine Calling. I surrender my mind, my emotions, and my instincts to Your refining process. Lead me in wisdom and humility, that I may discern the enemy's tactics and overcome them by the POWER of Your Divine Truth. In Jesus' Name I pray, Amen.

PRAYER OVERRIDE 6

The Mark of Begging

Most Holy and Loving Father, I come before You in humility, recognizing my place in Earthen Vessel shaped by Your hands, and yet vulnerable to the temptations and trials of this world. I acknowledge Your sovereignty and wisdom, knowing that nothing in my heart or circumstances escapes Your notice. In Your presence, I bring to You *The Mark of Begging*, this subtle force that preys upon my fears, insecurities, and longings for connection.

Lord, I confess that in my deepest moments of need, I have sometimes crossed the line between asking for help and begging for it. I have found myself reaching out, not in confidence or mutual respect, but in desperation, forsaking my dignity and the dignity of others. I see now that this pattern of pleading is often manipulated by the enemy, who exploits my vulnerability to sow seeds of dependency, distraction, and disappointment within my Spirit.

Father, I thank You for the community You have placed around me, for the truth that I am not meant to walk this path alone. I recognize that healthy, Spirit-led requests for support can foster unity, build character, and strengthen relationships. Yet, I also realize that when I beg, when I try to control others or force outcomes, I violate the Spiritual Principle of free will that You Yourself have honored in Your Divine Creation. Even You, O God, do not override the free will of Your children, and so I must not attempt to do so with others.

Forgive me, Lord, for every time I have allowed fear or insecurity to drive me into patterns of manipulation or emotional pleading. Cleanse me of the need to control, and free me from every illusion that binds my heart to cycles of dependency. Teach me the profound difference between asking and begging. Help me to approach others with clarity, respect, and gratitude, always honoring their autonomy and intentions, just as You honor mine.

Holy Spirit, guide me to recognize the true needs within me, and empower me to bring them first to You in prayer. Let me listen for Your instructions, document my concerns with honesty, and communicate with clarity and kindness, regardless of whether I am accepted or rejected. Cover me with the Blood of Jesus, and let Your guidance be my constant companion. Shape my character so that I remain Christlike in every interaction, supportive to others, and grateful for every blessing.

Lord, I acknowledge that not everyone will walk beside me, and not everyone will offer help. Give me the wisdom and discernment to recognize when to let go, to save my energy for what truly matters in Your Divine Eye. Also, prompt me when to release any resentment or bitterness that might arise from unmet expectations. Remind me that my worth and Divine Provisions come from You, not from the responses of others.

I surrender the urge to chase after those who have chosen not to stand with me. Instead, I ask You to surround me with those whose actions match their words, who offer help freely and wholeheartedly. Protect me from the schemes of the enemy, who seeks to aggravate my Spirit and disturb my peace through disappointment or rejection.

Father, grant me the resolve to keep my hands and heart blessed, even when misunderstood or overlooked. Let me always strive to stay on the righteous side of every encounter, and to repent quickly when I step onto the path of unrighteousness. Search my heart for any hidden motives of control or manipulation, and purify me from within.

Help me to DISCERN and TEST the Spirit behind every mark I encounter, especially when dealing with the Spirit of Compromise, Conformity, or Rebellion that seeks to distance me from You. Make me vigilant against the systems of control that the world parades as progress. Let my loyalty be a mark of unwavering devotion to You, not to anything or anyone that opposes Your Divine Will for me or mankind.

I stand on the truth of Your Word, remembering the WARNING and the PROMISE. That submission to anything You hate brings destruction from within, and obedience to You brings patience, faith, and everlasting life. May I keep Your commandments and the faith of Jesus, resisting every Spirit that seeks to beguile or enslave me and those I hold dear to my heart.

Lead me daily in the path of humility, gratitude, and Holy Confidence, *As It Pleases You*. May I always recognize my need, pray about it, listen for Your Sacred Voice, *Spirit to Spirit*, and cover myself with the Blood of Jesus. Let kindness, patience, and Christlike love be my response in all things, as the Holy Spirit goes before me to guide and illuminate my path. I give You thanks for every lesson, every test, and every opportunity to honor You. In Jesus' Name I pray, Amen.

PRAYER OVERRIDE 7

The Mark of Blindness

Heavenly Father, I come before You with a humbled heart, seeking to understand Your Spiritual Mysteries of Divine Sight and Perception that You alone ordained for my Heaven on Earth Experience. I recognize that, in this world, I am often tempted to believe that what I see is all there is, that clarity is found only with the eyes. Yet, You remind me that the deepest truths are not visible to the natural eye but are discerned in the Realm of the Spirit. Lord, I confess that I have sometimes relied too heavily on my limited understanding, missing the greater reality that lies beyond what is seen.

Today, I boldly ask You to deliver me from *The Mark of Blindness*, in the Name of Jesus. Strip away every layer of illusion, denial, and avoidance that clouds my sense of good judgment and keeps me from walking in Divine Clarity, *As It Pleases You*. Where I have ignored my problems, chosen the easier path of distractions, or allowed my fears and hang-ups to govern my responses, forgive me. Guide me to face every challenge head-on through the strength of Your Spirit, trusting that avoidance only deepens my struggles.

Father, I acknowledge the profound danger of my Spiritual Blindness, along with the inability to see myself, others, and even You with the eyes of truth. Please open my eyes to my own truths, my weaknesses, my hidden traumas, and the realities that I have resisted confronting. Teach me to reflect deeply on my words, actions, desires, and thoughts, so that I do not remain trapped in cycles of misunderstanding and missed opportunities for Spiritual Growth. Remind me that Divine Vision or Insight is not a privilege of the human eyes but a Divine Gift granted to those who seek You, *As It Pleases You*.

Lord, as You healed the blind man in Bethsaida, You revealed that perception can be distorted even as healing begins. I ask You to touch my Spiritual Eyes again and again until I see with full clarity. Where I have seen men as trees walking, correct my vision. Let me not be satisfied with partial sight but press on for the fullness of understanding that only You can provide.

Empower me with the faith of the woman who reached out to touch the hem of Your garment, believing in her heart that wholeness was possible because of Your presence. Let desperation for You override every doubt, every failed attempt, and every disappointment. Teach me to draw deeply from the well of faith within, connecting *Spirit to Spirit* with Your Healing Power, knowing that my greatest breakthroughs come when I trust You completely.

Help me to override every veil of blindness by aligning my mind and heart with Your Divine Will. Show me how to examine myself honestly, to challenge my perceptions, and to embrace correction as a mark of Spiritual maturity. Let my life be a living testimony of transformation, rooted and grounded in Your love, mercy, and truth. Where pride, selfishness, or cultural indoctrination has clouded my sense of good judgment, uproot these things and plant in me a Spirit of humility, wisdom, and discernment.

Father, grant me the courage to function in the Spirit of Excellence even when the way ahead seems uncertain. May I embrace the challenge of seeing with the Divine Eye of the Spirit, moving beyond surface realities to discern the deeper things You wish to reveal. Let my relationships, my decisions, and my testimony be shaped by the clarity and compassion that flow from Your heart.

In moments when You call me to silence, may I exercise discretion and wisdom, allowing my TESTIMONY to speak through my life rather than my lips. Teach me to wait for Your Divine Timing, to share only as You lead, and to walk in obedience, knowing that VICTORY is Spiritually Sealed by the Blood of the Lamb and the word of my Testimony.

Lord, I surrender every *Mark of Blindness* within me to Your healing hands. Remove every veil, every distortion, and every obstacle that keeps me from seeing, knowing, and doing Your Divine Will, *As It Pleases You*. Fill me with the fullness of Your Spirit, granting me Divine Clarity, unwavering faith, and a heart continually aligned with Your Divine Purpose and Spiritual Blueprint. In Jesus' Name I pray, Amen.

PRAYER OVERRIDE 8

The Mark of Brokenness

Gracious Heavenly Father, I come before You acknowledging *The Mark of Brokenness* in my life, seeking Your Divine Wisdom to understand its depths and purposes. In the Eye of God, I know that brokenness is not simply a matter of pain, but a Sacred Ground where vulnerability, victimhood, and overcoming converge, reflecting the tri-fold nature of my Spiritual Journey. I admit that I have often wavered between being overly independent and giving in to co-dependency, forgetting that my ultimate strength and healing come from You alone. Lord, help me to choose the path of humility, allowing brokenness to be transformed into the fertile soil where Your Spirit can bring forth new life for the Greater Good.

I confess that I have sometimes tried to hide my wounds or allowed the enemy to exploit my fears, insecurities, and past traumas. In those moments, I have felt the weight of despair, confusion, and isolation, believing my struggles would shackle me forever. Yet, Your Divine Word assures me that, when I surrender my brokenness, Your Grace, Mercy, and Healing become my shield. I thank You for the safety net of Your love, which turns even my deepest pain into stepping stones toward Divine Greatness and Supernatural Reliance on You.

Father, I ask that You expose every lie I have believed about my worth, my purpose, and my future. Let every element of brokenness in me, whether rooted in pride, fear, doubt, or self-reliance, be brought into the light of Your truth. Where I have grieved Your Spirit by withdrawing or becoming indifferent, restore in me a Spirit of connection and belonging. Remind me that I am created for relationship, not only with others, but first and foremost with You. Just as the Holy Trinity models ONENESS, grant me a deeper understanding of relational harmony so that I may reflect Your nature in every aspect of my life.

Lord, give me the courage to develop a *Spirit to Spirit* relationship with You. Cover me with the Blood of Jesus as Spiritual Atonement and usher in the presence of the Holy Spirit to guide my every thought, word, and action. Teach me to repent, forgive, meditate, and pray, aligning my life with the Word of God. Empower me to own my truth, cast off deception, and walk in humility. Let the Fruits of the Spirit and Christlike Character traits become the hallmarks of my daily life in the Spirit of Truth.

I ask for Divine Wisdom to Spiritually Discern the wise from the unwise, the innocent from the foolish, and the wicked from the just, both in myself and others. Let me not answer folly with folly, nor walk in the path of the wicked, but remain steadfast in righteousness, *As It Pleases You*. May I always seek Your Divine Instructions while growing in learning, obedience, and understanding as Your Word commands.

Father, I recognize that my weaknesses are opportunities for Your strength to be perfected in me. Do not let me run from the vicissitudes of life, but instead grant me the self-awareness, self-control, and self-motivation needed to grow. Let the Fruits of the Spirit flourish within me so that I may relate to others with compassion, patience, and love. Keep me accountable, humble, and obedient, always striving to reflect the character of Christ in every circumstance.

When I am tempted to get in Your way or hinder my own progress, remind me to surrender fully. Teach me to align my Mind, Body, Soul, and Spirit *As It Pleases You*, knowing that Your Divine Purpose will prevail regardless of my resistance. Let me develop the Divine Intelligence and people skills necessary to thrive in my relationships. Help me to maintain a work-in-progress mentality, trusting that You are faithful to complete the good work You have begun in me.

Father, I thank You for never leaving me alone in my brokenness. Even when I grieve Your Spirit or falter in my faith, Your Divine Grace and Mercy will cover me regardless. Remind me that, no matter how hard life pushes me toward perfection, only You can reverse engineer my brokenness and bring forth wholeness. Give me the strength to get out of Your way and my own way, so that You may do what only You can do.

I present my brokenness, my pain, and my imperfections to You now, trusting that You will use every piece as part of my Testimony for the Greater Good of mankind. Let my life be a TESTAMENT to Your transforming power, Your relentless love, and Your unwavering faithfulness. In Jesus' Name I pray, Amen.

PRAYER OVERRIDE 9

The Mark of Busyness

Heavenly Father, I come before You with a heart heavy from the weight of busyness, asking for Your guidance and intervention. In a world that glorifies constant activity, I confess that I have often mistaken motion for meaning and productivity for purpose. I have run from task to task, chasing after accomplishments and accolades, yet my Spirit sometimes feels empty, confused, frustrated, and lost. I have allowed my life to become filled with distractions, obligations, and endless to-do lists, often neglecting what truly matters. I have found that what matters and what is missing is my *Spirit to Spirit* relationship with You, *As It Pleases You*. Which is needed to get to the Divine Purpose You have Divinely Written on the tablet of my heart with a specific BLUEPRINT.

Lord, I admit that I have sometimes pursued recognition, success, and validation from others, losing sight of the deeper truth that my worth is rooted in Your love and calling. I have measured my value by what I achieve and possess, rather than by who I am in You. Forgive me for the times I have allowed *The Mark of Busyness* to obscure my vision, cloud my mind, and pull me away from Your Holy Presence. I surrender my frantic efforts and restless striving, asking You to realign my life according to Your Divine Blueprint.

Father, help me to pause and reflect on my real reason for being. Teach me to seek Your Divine Will above my own plans, to prioritize what PLEASES You over what inflates my ego or satisfies the fleeting desires of my flesh. Let me not be entangled in cycles of fruitless activity, but instead, show me how to walk in step with Your Spirit, finding fulfillment and strength in doing what You have called me to do.

Grant me the wisdom to discern the difference between meaningful pursuits and empty busyness. Help me to recognize when my actions are motivated by fear, pride, or a need to prove myself, and give me the courage to let go of all that stands in the way of Your peace. Fill my days with intentionality, teaching me to manage my time as a GIFT from You, not as a master over me. Remind me that You are the Creator of time itself and that, in Your Divine Will, all things find their proper order and place.

Father, I ask You to reveal where I have allowed busyness to become a distraction, a weapon in the hands of the adversary, or a substitute for true connection with You and others. Where I have ignored my vulnerabilities, neglected areas of growth, or avoided honest self-examination, awaken me to the shadows that threaten my well-being. Teach me to be self-aware, to reflect regularly on my character, habits, relationships, thoughts, words, and motives, so that I may detect and address weaknesses before they become stumbling blocks.

Lord, help me to reclaim my time and align my pursuits with Your values. Give me the grace to say no to what is unnecessary and to delegate or release commitments that do not serve Your purpose for my life. Let my faith, works, and Blessings speak for themselves, always pointing back to Your Glory and not to my own achievements. May my life be marked not by busyness, but by balance, Divine Balance to be exact. All of which is held together by faith, joy, peace, love, and fulfillment flowing from my relationship with You, with myself, and with others.

Remind me that true Blessings come from You alone, not from self-deception, worldly approval, or fleeting gain. Keep me from boasting or comparing myself to others, and instead, teach me to walk humbly, giving thanks for every good thing You provide. Let my works be a Testimony of faith, integrity, and accountability, always rooted in the Fruits of the Spirit and the character of Christ Jesus.

Father, as I seek to override *The Mark of Busyness*, help me to engage in meaningful preparation and honest reflection. Show me what needs adjusting, maintaining, or growing in my life. Bring to light any neglected relationships or routines, and grant me the wisdom to nurture and strengthen the foundation of my faith. Make me vigilant to recognize the subtle ways the enemy seeks to distract or derail me, so that I may remain anchored in Your truth and equipped to face adversity with confidence.

Above all, Lord, help me to pursue balance and fulfillment as You have designed, not as the world defines. Let my Spirit find rest and renewal in Your presence, *Spirit to Spirit*, knowing that my worth and purpose are secure in You. May I always honor You with my time, talents, and treasures, living each day as a reflection of Your Divine Love, Mercy, and Grace. In Jesus' Name I pray, Amen.

PRAYER OVERRIDE 10

The Mark of Collapse

Heavenly Father, I come before You in humility and awe, recognizing that *The Mark of Collapse* can shake the very foundations of my faith, my resilience, and my clarity. In a world filled with overwhelming pressures and conflicts, I acknowledge that I cannot navigate the storms of life in my own strength. Lord, I confess that there are moments when the weight of my burdens, fears, and disappointments threatens to overwhelm me, leaving me feeling vulnerable and exposed. Yet, I trust that in Your hands, every collapse is an opportunity for Divine Intervention, Growth, and Restoration, as You see fit.

Father, I ask that You open my eyes to the warnings and lessons embedded within the seasons and cycles of my life. Help me to recognize when I am straying from Your Divine Will, especially when pride, disobedience, or blame seek to take root in my heart. Remind me that true Spiritual Authority and Divine Dominion only flourish when I walk in humility and obedience, placing You at the center of my every thought and action. Where I have misused my free will or attempted to manipulate Your Divine Order for selfish gain, I repent and seek Your forgiveness.

Lord, I thank You for Your promise that when the righteous cry out, You hear and deliver them from all troubles. I call upon You in the day of trouble, knowing that You alone are able to collapse any system, structure, or circumstance that stands in the way of Your Predestined Purpose for my life. Even when You allow challenges to remain, help me to embrace the lessons You teach, to grow in strength and resilience, and to align myself with Your Divine Plan for the Greater Good of all mankind.

Father, I ask for discernment to understand the root causes of collapse in my life, whether they stem from doubt, fear, instability, or Spiritual Weariness. Reveal to me the subtle tactics of the adversary that seek to sow discord, contention, and anxiety. Grant me vigilance to recognize the signs of internal strife before they escalate, and give me the wisdom and courage to address conflicts with compassion and self-control.

Guard my heart against the things You hate, such as pride, deceit, wicked plans, and discord. Help me to rule over my own Spirit, that I may not become like a city without walls, vulnerable to collapse and defeat. Teach me to be proactive in reflection, to ask myself the hard questions, and to maintain Christlike Character even in the face of adversity. Let my faith, hope, trust, and love be tested and refined, knowing that You are always working things out for my good and Your glory.

Lord, I surrender every area of my life where collapse threatens to undermine my faith. Where I am weak, be my strength. Where I am blind, grant me sight. Where I am weary, renew my Spirit. Fill me with integrity, wisdom, and humility so that I may approach every challenge with Your authority and peace. Empower me to recognize my limitations and to call on You for Spiritual Backup, knowing that victory is not mine alone but belongs to the Holy Trinity at work in and through me.

Father, I renounce any Spirit of superficiality, greed, or compromise that would erode the values of Your Kingdom. Keep me from seeking recognition, profit, or power at the expense of truth, mercy, integrity, and love. Remind me to serve others in the Spirit of Christ, offering healing, wisdom, and prayer freely as You have given to me. Let my life be a Testimony to the power of Your grace and the depth of Your compassion.

As I stand in the midst of life's unpredictable storms, I place my trust in You, believing that every collapse can become a catalyst for deeper faith, renewed purpose, and greater alignment according to Your Divine Will. Strengthen my resolve to persevere, to learn, and to glorify You in every circumstance. May I never lose sight of Your Divine Presence, Your Spiritually Sealed Promises, and Your unfailing love. In Jesus' Name I pray, Amen.

PRAYER OVERRIDE 11

The Mark of Colorism

Heavenly Father, I come before You with a contrite heart, lifting up the heavy burden of *The Mark of Colorism* that has wounded so many and sown discord among Your people. Lord, You have made each of us in Your image, beautiful in the diversity of our skin, our cultures, and our stories. Yet I confess that I have witnessed, and at times participated in, the silent and insidious sin of colorism that divides rather than unites, that wounds rather than heals. I repent for every thought, word, or deed, known or unknown, that has perpetuated this mark, and I ask for Your forgiveness and cleansing.

Father, I acknowledge that colorism is a tool of the enemy, a demonic force that seeks to fragment communities, families, and hearts. I renounce every lie that attaches worth or value to the shade of a person's skin. I reject every stereotype that pits brother against brother, sister against sister, or elevates one above another for reasons that are not of You. Lord, search my heart and expose any hidden bias or prejudice that lingers within me. Replace it with the truth of Your unconditional love, that I may see others as You see them, worthy, valuable, and beloved.

Lord Jesus, You have called me to live without partiality, to reflect Your justice and mercy, and to honor the Image of God in every person. Where I have failed to speak up against colorism or have remained silent in the face of injustice, give me the courage to be an agent of change. Let my words and actions promote unity, compassion, and restoration within my community and beyond. Remind me that silence can be complicity, and empower me to confront this evil with truth and love.

Holy Spirit, fill me with discernment and wisdom as I navigate conversations and relationships shaped by the scars of colorism. Help me to dismantle every stronghold of pride, insecurity, or self-hatred that colorism has built, both within myself and in others. Grant me the humility to listen, to learn, and to walk in empathy. Reveal to me the ways in which I can uplift, affirm, and honor others, regardless of their skin tone or status.

Father, I pray for healing over the deep wounds caused by colorism; the wounds that manifest as insecurity, low self-esteem, distrust, anger, and despair. Pour out Your restoring grace over every heart and mind that has been damaged by this evil. Break the chains of generational pain and replace them with the Spirit of Acceptance, belonging, and hope. Let Your love dissolve every yoke of shame, comparison, and judgment, so that joy and peace may flourish in their place.

Lord, help me to remember that material gain, status, or outward appearance are never measures of character or worth in Your Divine Eye. Teach me to value what You value: love, justice, mercy, and truth. Let Galatians 3:28 be the banner over my life and relationships, reminding me that in Christ, we are all one. Remove from me any Spirit of superiority or inferiority rooted in colorism, and root me deeply in my identity as Your child.

Father, give me the wisdom to release what does not belong to me, to make restitution where I have harmed others, and to pursue reconciliation as a vessel of Your peace. Where division has prevailed, sow seeds of unity and restoration. Where confusion and oppression have reigned, pour out clarity and liberation. Let my life reflect the PROMISE that You defend the oppressed and restore STOLEN LEGACIES in Your time and way.

Holy Spirit, sustain me in the ongoing work of overcoming colorism. Empower me with faith, courage, and perseverance to stand for truth, to challenge injustice, and to overcome every mark that is not from You. Let me walk in humility, wisdom, and Christlike love, always mindful that Your Divine Presence is at work in every story, every person, and every struggle.

Father, I surrender to Your refining work in my heart. May *The Mark of Colorism* be forever broken in my life and community, replaced by the Spirit of unity, equality, and genuine love. Help me to get out of my own way and to align with Your purpose, so that I may be an instrument of healing and transformation in the world. In Jesus' Name I pray, Amen.

PRAYER OVERRIDE 12

The Mark of Comparison

Heavenly Father, I come before You sincerely, laying down the heavy burden of *The Mark of Comparison* that has too often clouded my Spirit and dimmed my understanding of my worth. Lord, I recognize that You have created me uniquely, with a purpose and destiny that are divinely tailored for me alone. Yet, I confess that the enemy has sought to distort my vision by tempting me to measure myself against others, breeding feelings of inadequacy, jealousy, envy, and discontentment within my heart.

    Father, I repent for every moment I have doubted my value, questioned my identity, or allowed the opinions or successes of others to overshadow the GIFTS You have placed within me. Forgive me for the times I have harbored resentment, boasted in self-seeking, or entertained bitterness because of comparison. I acknowledge Your Word in 2 Corinthians 10:12 and James 3:14-16, affirming that comparison and envy open doors to confusion and every evil thing, and I do not want these things to take root in my life.

    Lord, help me to understand that my journey is not of my own, and that Your plans for me are good and purposeful. Teach me to celebrate the victories and blessings of others, knowing that their success does not diminish my worth or limit Your ability to BLESS me or them. Deliver me from the trap of measuring myself by the standards of this world or the expectations of others. Instead, draw my focus to the marks of the Lord Jesus, as Paul writes in Galatians 6:17. Let me be marked by faith, perseverance, humility, and love, not by comparison or competition.

    Holy Spirit, reveal to me the subtle ways that comparison tries to creep into my thoughts, words, and actions. Give me discernment to recognize when I am tempted to diminish my own gifts or amplify the shortcomings of others. Fill me with gratitude, contentment, and a Spirit of Compassion for myself and those around me. Help me to align my heart and values with Your Divine Will, to reflect honestly on my habits, motives, and relationships, and to uproot any seeds of discord or self-deception that comparison has sown.

Father, I ask for healing in every area where *The Mark of Comparison* has wounded my self-esteem, distorted my judgment, or hindered my relationships. Break every cycle of validation-seeking, perfectionism, gossip, or chaos that has arisen from my struggle to feel as if I am enough. Restore my sense of purpose and worth, reminding me that I am fearfully and wonderfully made, and that Your Spirit is at work within me to shape me into the Image of Christ.

Lord, empower me to walk in wholeness, integrity, and humility. Let me be quick to celebrate the strengths and achievements of others, quick to forgive any resentment, and quick to extend mercy and encouragement. Guard my heart from projecting my shortcomings onto others, from excluding those who should be included, or from thriving off of external validation. Teach me to find my joy, identity, and fulfillment in You alone.

May my life be a Testimony of overcoming *The Mark of Comparison*. Let Your Spirit continually remind me that my value is not determined by what I lack, but by who I am in You. Help me to be a vessel of encouragement, unity, and love, uplifting others as I embrace my own journey. May I always wear the marks of Christ, living as an overcomer and pointing others to the freedom found only in You. In Jesus' Name I pray, Amen.

PRAYER OVERRIDE 13

The Mark of Competitiveness

Heavenly Father, I come before You with a heart that longs for transformation, honesty, and the fullness of Your truth. As I reflect on *The Mark of Competitiveness*, I recognize how easily it can entangle my Spirit, working hand in hand with *The Mark of Comparison*. Like Esau and Jacob, these forces wrestle within me, competing for dominance and shaping the way I see myself and others. I acknowledge that, without Your guidance, competitiveness can become a double-edged sword, driving me to strive not for Your glory but for the applause of men and the fleeting crowns of this world.

Lord, I confess that there are times when I have measured my worth against others, allowing feelings of inadequacy or pride to take root in my heart. I see how quickly the desire to win, to be first, or to be acknowledged can overshadow my calling to humility, service, and love. I remember Your Word in 1 Corinthians 9:24-27 that urges me to run the race in such a way as to obtain a crown that does not perish, to discipline my body and bring it into subjection, lest I myself become disqualified. I pray that You would help me to embrace the Spirit of Self-control, to run not with uncertainty, but with purpose and conviction that come from Your Spirit.

As I pursue my goals, passions, and ambitions, teach me to maintain a heart of humility and a mindset that seeks the well-being of others. May I strive for excellence without falling into the trap of arrogance or entitlement. Strengthen me to encourage and uplift those around me, to celebrate their victories as my own, and to offer support when they stumble. Help me to remember Ecclesiastes 4:9-10, that two are better than one, and that together we can accomplish far more than we ever could alone.

Father, I ask for discernment to recognize when competitiveness is becoming unhealthy or when it is being used by the enemy as a tool for division, discouragement, or compromise. When the pressure mounts, when my emotions threaten to overtake me, and when my past experiences or imagined dangers bombard my mind, may Your Spirit intercede on my behalf. I confess that I do not always have control over my thoughts, reactions, or even the chemicals in my brain, but I trust in Your Divine Power to bring my Mind, Body, Soul, and Spirit into alignment with Your Divine Will.

Lord, unlock the places in my psyche that are bound by fear, insecurity, or past trauma. Let Divine Training shape my character, not just through what I can see, but through the deep, hidden work of Your Spirit within me. Lead me through my own desert experiences, and purge from me anything that keeps me from entering into the fullness of Your Divine Promises. Remind me that true victory is not found in outperforming others, but in becoming the person You have called me to be.

I lift up those who struggle with anxiety, stress, and the lingering effects of unhealthy competition. Whether they are athletes, soldiers, business leaders, children, or anyone else, I pray for healing and restoration in their minds and hearts. May the alarm systems within us, the Amygdala and all its complex workings, be brought under the gentle authority of Your Spirit, so that we are not slaves to fear, anger, or the need to prove ourselves.

Father, equip me to recognize the signs of a Competitive Spirit within myself. When I am tempted to degrade others, to chase titles, to avoid teamwork, or to base my value solely on achievements, gently convict me. When I struggle to celebrate others, when I fear being surpassed, when I am suspicious, or when I engage in negative self-talk, draw me back to the truth of who I am in Christ Jesus. Help me to resist *The Mark of Compromise* that so often follows unchecked competitiveness. Guard my heart against the subtle lies of self-deception. I acknowledge that lying to myself is a poison that erodes authenticity, destroys relationships, and clouds my sense of good judgment. Grant me the courage to face my uncomfortable truths, to admit my mistakes, and to grow in humility. Let honesty with You, with myself, and with others become my shield and my refuge.

Search me, O God, and know my heart. Try me and know my anxieties. See if there is any wicked way in me, and lead me in the way everlasting. May Your Spirit bring to light anything within me that needs to be surrendered, healed, or transformed. Father, I surrender my ambitions, my drive, and my desire to win at all costs. May my competitive nature be balanced by a Spirit of grace, humility, and wisdom. Let me not wander aimlessly, but instead walk purposefully in the path You have set before me. May my life bear the mark of Christ, not the mark of unhealthy competitiveness. In Jesus' Name I pray, Amen.

PRAYER OVERRIDE 14

The Mark of Compromise

Gracious and Almighty Father, I bow before You today with a heart that longs to remain pure and steadfast, seeking Your Divine Wisdom and guidance as I confront the Spirit of the Nicolaitan. Your Word warns against teachings and practices that lead to compromise, pride, and separation from Your truth. I acknowledge that the Spirit of the Nicolaitan represents a mindset that seeks to divide, dominate, and distort the purity of Your Gospel. It promotes Spiritual Hierarchy, abuses of authority, and a blending of worldly values with the sacred teachings of Christ.

Lord, I confess that at times I have allowed pride, self-righteousness, or the desire for control to influence my actions and attitudes. I ask You to search my heart and remove any trace of this Spirit that seeks to elevate self above service, power above humility, or tradition above relationship with You. Help me to recognize when I am tempted to compromise the teachings of Christ for personal gain, comfort, or the approval of others.

By Your Spirit, fill me with discernment to identify and reject any doctrine or practice that undermines the lordship of Jesus or diminishes the unity of Your Body. Teach me to walk in humility, always placing others before myself and seeking to build up rather than tear down. Let my leadership and influence be marked by love, service, and a Spirit of gentleness, never by dominance or manipulation.

As I reflect on *The Mark of Compromise*, I am reminded of how subtle and deceptive it can be, often slipping into my thoughts and actions without my awareness. Your Word in Proverbs 21:2 warns me that every way of a man is right in his own eyes, but You, O Lord, weigh the hearts. I confess that I cannot always see where I have compromised, for my own understanding is limited and sometimes clouded by pride, fear, or self-justification.

Father, I humbly invite the Holy Trinity into every decision I make, every agreement I enter, and every relationship I nurture. I ask that You help me align my life with Your Word, measuring all things by the Fruits of the Spirit and the example of Christ. By Your Spirit, teach me to discern what is truly good, right, and PLEASING in Your sight. Where I have fallen short, open my eyes and convict my heart, so that I may turn away from anything that does not honor You.

Lord, I realize that compromise can sometimes appear wise or necessary, especially in a world that prizes tolerance, negotiation, and the art of agreement. Yet I know that if You are not at the center of my choices, I risk surrendering my standards, beliefs, integrity, and identity to the shifting winds of circumstance and opinion. Help me to know not only what I am giving and what I am taking, but also why I am doing so. Guard me from the snares of the enemy, who seeks to exploit my weaknesses and lead me into agreements that erode my character, diminish my values, and detach me from Your Divine Purpose for my life.

Spirit of Truth, search my heart and expose any area where compromise has taken root. Where I have excused small sins, rationalized poor behavior, or justified choices that do not align with Your Divine Will, shine Your light and bring conviction. Where I have allowed fear, insecurity, convenience, or the desire for approval to influence my actions, forgive me and strengthen my resolve. Remind me that the most dangerous compromises are those that go unnoticed, quietly corroding the foundation of my faith and character.

Lord, I ask for wisdom to recognize the difference between healthy cooperation and unhealthy compromise. Grant me discernment to know when to yield for the sake of peace and when to stand firm for the sake of righteousness. Help me to pursue unity without sacrificing truth, to show grace without abandoning conviction, and to be flexible without becoming double-minded. When I am tempted to exchange my Spiritual Inheritance for temporary gain, as Esau did, remind me of my eternal value of obedience and faithfulness to You.

Father, I pray for courage to walk in integrity, even when it costs me comfort, popularity, or acceptance. Let me not be swayed by the opinions of others or the pressures of this world, but let me anchor my soul in Your unchanging truth. Where I have compromised in my relationships, my work, my words, or my worship, restore me. Give me the humility to confess my faults, seek forgiveness, and make things right.

Help me to be vigilant, for the enemy is cunning and relentless, always seeking to dilute my convictions and distort my perceptions. May I be found watchful, prayerful, and clothed in the full armor of God, so that I can withstand every scheme that comes to undermine my faith. When I am weary, reassure me of Your presence and power. When I am uncertain, remind me that Your Spirit guides me into all truth.

Lord, I ask that You surround me with godly counsel and accountability, people who will speak truth in love and encourage me to stay the course. Help me to value self-examination and alignment with Your Word above the fleeting approval of men. Let my standards always be Christlike, measured by the Fruits of the Spirit: Love, Joy, Peace, Patience, Kindness, Goodness, Faithfulness, Gentleness, and Self-Control.

Father, I surrender my heart, mind, and will to You. Weigh my motives and purify my desires. Where I am tempted to lower my standards or stray from Your path for the sake of convenience, success, or comfort, draw me back by the gentle leading of Your Spirit. Let me find my greatest satisfaction in PLEASING You, knowing that Your approval is worth far more than anything this world can offer. I pray for the courage to stand firm against Spiritual Compromise and false teachings. Give me the strength to uphold Your truth, even when it is unpopular or misunderstood. Surround me with wise and faithful Believers who encourage me to remain steadfast and accountable. Help me to cherish the simplicity and purity of devotion to Christ, refusing to be drawn into systems or structures that exalt human authority over the guidance of Your Spirit.

I appreciate the example of Jesus, who came not to be served but to serve, and who laid down His life in obedience to Your Divine Will. May I follow in His footsteps, embracing humility, integrity, and sacrificial love in all that I do, say, and become. I surrender every area of my life to Your lordship, asking You to cleanse me from all that does not honor You. Let my words, actions, and motives be PLEASING in Your sight, and may I always seek to glorify You above all else.

Above all, my Lord, with no shame attached, I surrender all of my ambitions, motives, and desires to You, *As It Pleases You*. Cleanse my heart and renew my mind, so that I may walk in integrity, love, peace, and truth, superseding all human understanding.

Thank You for Your patience, mercy, and unfailing love. Thank You for giving me the power to overcome every mark that seeks to stain my soul. May my life be marked by an unwavering DEVOTION to You, characterized by integrity, conviction, and a Spirit-led pursuit of HOLINESS. In Jesus' Name I pray, Amen.

PRAYER OVERRIDE 15

The Mark of Confusion

Heavenly Father, I come before You with a heart longing for clarity, peace, and discernment in the midst of the confusion that surrounds me. In this age of information overload and relentless distractions, I often find myself overwhelmed by conflicting voices and ideologies. Sometimes I struggle to limit my intake and set boundaries, and I admit that I do not always question the source of what I consume. I recognize how easy it is to be drawn into endless debates, forgetting to approach others with curiosity, humility, and a willingness to listen and learn, *As It Pleases You.*

Lord, Your Word in 1 Corinthians 14:33 reminds me that You are not the author of confusion, but of peace, as in all the churches of the saints. I confess that I am sometimes swept away by uncertainty, doubt, and disorientation. I second-guess my beliefs, question myself, and find it difficult to make sound decisions. I am aware that these moments of confusion can open the door to psychological manipulation and deception. For this reason, I choose to heed Your command in 1 John 4:1 to TEST the Spirit, to EXAMINE what is truly from You, and to REJECT all falsehood.

Father, I ask for the wisdom to discern genuine truth from cleverly disguised lies. I pray for the courage to confront the deeper questions of my life, to seek the source of confusion, and to root myself firmly in Your unchanging Word. In a world full of enticing promises and alluring symbols of belonging, help me to remember that my ultimate allegiance is to You alone. Remind me that true peace, joy, love, patience, kindness, goodness, faithfulness, and self-control are GIFTS from Your Spirit, not commodities to be traded or purchased at the expense of my soul.

Lord, I acknowledge that the Mark of Confusion is not a distant threat, but a reality that seeks to undermine my sense of purpose and commitment. It is present in the choices I make, in the stories I tell myself, and in the moments when I ignore the gentle tug of conviction upon my conscience. I know that the enemy seeks to use confusion as a weapon, to keep me bogged down in shame, regret, and self-doubt. Help me to recognize when the past is being weaponized against me, and grant me the strength to release shame so that confusion cannot hold me captive.

Spirit of Truth, search the depths of my heart and reveal anything that feeds confusion within me. Where I have allowed resentment, unforgiveness, or distrust to take root, I ask for Your healing and restoration. Teach me to walk in self-control, to guard my thoughts, words, habits, actions, reactions, and desires, and to remain sensitive to Your Divine Guidance. When uncertainty arises, let it drive me to seek Your Divine Wisdom rather than to withdraw or rationalize away my discomfort or seek my own version of wisdom.

Father, I understand that my actions, thoughts, and words tell a story, and that the enemy can use my history to manipulate and destabilize me if I am not vigilant. I ask You to help me own my story, to remove the power of shame, and to stand firm in the freedom You have given me. Let me not be swayed by the shifting winds of opinion, nor paralyzed by indecision or fear. Instead, fill me with the confidence and assurance that come from knowing I am rooted in Christ Jesus, *As It Pleases You*.

Lord, when life becomes overwhelming, and I sense uncertainty tugging at my Spirit, remind me that You are with me. Help me to pause, seek Your Divine Presence, and listen for the gentle whispers of Your Voice, *Spirit to Spirit*. Grant me the grace to acknowledge my limitations as a human being and to rely on Your strength and wisdom rather than my own understanding. Keep me humble, teachable, and ever aware that apart from You I can do nothing.

I pray that You will surround me with wise counsel and godly community, people who will encourage me, challenge me, and help me to discern truth from error. Let my mind be renewed daily by Your Word, and let Your peace guard my heart against all confusion and chaos. May I be a vessel of clarity, unity, and steadfast faith in a world that desperately needs Your light.

Thank You for being my Spiritual Anchor and my Hidden Refuge in every storm. Thank You for the PROMISE that if I ask for Divine Wisdom, *As It Pleases You*, You will give it generously without finding fault. Thus, I choose to surrender every mark of confusion, every doubt, and every fear to You. Lead me on the path of clarity, purpose, and unwavering devotion. In Jesus' Name I pray, Amen.

PRAYER OVERRIDE 16

The Mark of Control

Heavenly Father, I come before You in humility and reverence, acknowledging that You alone are Sovereign over all creation. I thank You for Your unfailing love, Your Divine Wisdom, and Your ceaseless grace that guides me through every season of my life. Lord, I confess that in this world filled with the lure of instant gratification and the temptation to control every detail, my heart is often pulled toward taking the control from Your hands. I recognize the deep longing within me for perfection, order, and influence over people, places, and things, sometimes even at the expense of their free will, and I repent for every time I have tried to play God in my own life or in the lives of others.

Father, I acknowledge that true control belongs to You alone. Teach me to surrender my desire to orchestrate outcomes and to trust in Your perfect plan. Guard my heart from the pride that seeks to elevate my ways above Yours. Protect me from the Spirit of manipulation that masquerades as righteousness but is void of true Spiritual Discernment. Deliver me from any urge to impress others or to appear holier than I am, for You see the depths of my soul, and nothing is hidden from Your sight.

Holy Spirit, I ask You to search me and know me. Reveal to me any area where *The Mark of Control* has taken root in my thoughts, words, or actions. Uncover within me any tendency to micromanage, to dominate, to resist change, or to withhold trust from others. Let me not be blinded by my own ambitions or insecurities, but rather, grant me the clarity to discern the fruit in my life and in the lives of those around me. As Your Word declares, by their fruits we shall know them. Grant me the courage to examine my own fruit with honesty and humility.

Lord, I pray for wisdom to discern authenticity from pretense, especially when I encounter those who wear the mask of Spirituality yet walk in error, folly, and debauchery. Let me not be quick to judge or to point fingers, for I am not the final authority over anyone's soul or salvation. Instead, help me to walk in grace, allowing each person to play their role while I remain steadfast in my calling to feed Your precious sheep and to fulfill my Divine Assignment, *As It Pleases You*. Remind me that my role is not to control the narrative but to trust You with every outcome.

Father, I ask for the discipline to TEST the Spirit and to INSPECT the fruit, not as a critic but as a student in Your Spiritual Classroom. Let every encounter, including those with deception and manipulation, serve as lessons that perfect my discernment and sharpen my Spiritual Senses. May I learn not just from my victories but from my wounds and scars, knowing that through every battle, You are shaping me for a Greater Purpose and for the Greater Good.

Grant me an undivided heart, O God, one that is clothed in humility, quick to serve, and slow to speak. Let me multiply and produce fruit that glorifies Your name, rather than seeking validation or applause from others. Teach me to bring Divine Order wherever I go, to tame the beasts from within and around me, and to walk in the authority You have given me, covered in Spiritual Armor. While at the same time, being empowered and protected by a Legion of Angels.

Lord, as the lines between progress, revelation, and prophecy become increasingly blurred in this world, give me the Spiritual Vision to see as You see, the Spiritual Ears to hear as You hear, and the Spiritual Voice to speak as You speak. Moreover, help me to recognize the hidden forces that seek to derail my Divine Destiny or to awaken the beast from within. Let me not fall prey to Spiritual Amnesia or forget the Spiritual Principles, Laws, and Protocols that grant me Divine leverage over the enemy. Remind me, Lord, that my strength is found in obedience, humility, and love, not in control or perfection.

I ask that You expose every area of my life where *The Spirit of Control* may be operating. Break every chain of perfectionism, anxiety, stiffness, selfishness, lukewarmness, dullness, or pride that prevents me from fully surrendering to You. Lord, I renounce every tendency to blame, to criticize, to covet, or to operate in envy and jealousy. Free me from the idolatry of myself and the need to orchestrate outcomes to appear better than I am. Instead, let me be a Divine Vessel of Your peace, a reflection of Your love, and a witness to Your redemptive power at work within me.

May my life be marked not by control, but by surrender. May my words and actions testify to the freedom found in yielding to Your Spirit. Transform me by Your Word and renew my mind so that I may discern what is good, acceptable, and perfect in Your sight. In Jesus' Name I pray, Amen.

PRAYER OVERRIDE 17

The Mark of Coveting

Heavenly Father, I come before You with an open and searching heart, acknowledging that You alone are all-wise, all-seeing, and the true Judge of my motives. I thank You for Your boundless grace and mercy, for You know every longing and secret place within me. Lord, I confess that there are times when the Spirit of Coveting has crept into my heart, sometimes quietly, sometimes boldly, tempting me to crave what does not belong to me. I admit that I have compared myself to others, envied their blessings, or allowed feelings of lack or unworthiness to cloud my gratitude for all You have given me.

Father, in Your Divine Eye, coveting is not just a desire, but a reflection of my innermost struggles, insecurities, and sometimes even my woundedness. I recognize that coveting can lead me down a path of resentment, bitterness, and discontentment, poisoning my psyche and separating me from peace and purpose. I ask for Your forgiveness, Lord, for every time I have entertained thoughts or desires that were not aligned with Your Divine Will. Cleanse my heart from all types of envy, jealousy, and unhealthy longings. Break every chain of comparison, and set me free from the prison of wanting what is not meant for me.

Holy Spirit, I invite You to search the depths and corners of my psyche. Reveal to me the ROOTS and SEEDS of my coveting, whether they stem from feelings of inadequacy, rejection, trauma, or a lack of trust in You or Your Divine Provisions. Help me to see every trigger and to confront it with truth and courage. Where I have doubted my worth, remind me that I am fearfully and wonderfully made. Where I have craved recognition or status, remind me that my true identity is found in You alone. Where I have been tempted to pursue what belongs to another, give me the humility and wisdom to step back and honor the boundaries You have set.   Lord, teach me to celebrate the blessings and successes of others with a pure heart. Let my words and actions reflect genuine joy for their victories, knowing that there is no lack in Your Kingdom. Help me to bless and not resent, to congratulate and not covet, to share in the joy of my brothers and sisters as one body, united in love.

Father, I ask that You dismantle every false belief that tells me I need more to be complete. Protect me from the subtle traps of social comparison, materialism, and the endless pursuit of status. Guard my heart from the influences of this age that seek to enslave me to desires that are temporary and empty. I am reminded that my TRUE TREASURE is in You, and that all good things come from Your hand, in Your Divine Timing, and according to Your Blueprinted Purpose.

Holy Spirit, when I am faced with those who covet what I have, help me to respond with grace, kindness, and wisdom. Let me not return envy with pride, jealousy, or arrogance, but rather, empower me to walk in humility, seeking peace and understanding. Teach me to recognize the pain behind their longing, and let my life be a TESTIMONY of contentment, gratitude, and the joy that comes from trusting in You. May I never hold tightly to what I possess, but be willing to share and to BLESS as You have BLESSED me.

Lord, I confess that coveting can be a warning sign of deeper unrest within me. Help me to use these moments as opportunities for self-examination, repentance, and growth. May I never ignore the signals of the Spirit, but instead be quick to turn to You for healing and restoration. Let me not allow the stress and anxiety of unfulfilled desires to poison my body or Spirit, but grant me the peace that surpasses all understanding.

Father, I pray for the strength to pursue righteousness over recognition, purpose over possession, and integrity over image. Remind me that true greatness is found not in what I acquire, but in how I love, serve, and honor You. If I have ever been a stumbling block to others by flaunting my blessings or boasting in my achievements, forgive me and teach me to walk in humility and quiet confidence.

Lord, I thank You for the second chances You give me to make amends for the times I have fallen short or dropped the ball. Grant me the courage to confront my hidden idols, to renounce every selfish ambition, and to reclaim my Divine Birthright as a Kingdom Citizen committed to Your Divine Will and Ways, *As It Pleases You*. Let me not allow the Spirit of Coveting to steal my legacy, my peace, or my trust in You. Help me to raise up an empire within; a life built on gratitude, contentment, and unwavering faith. I lay every desire, every longing, every hidden craving at Your feet, Lord. Purify my motives and align my heart with Yours. May *The Mark of Coveting* have no place in my life. Instead, let my life be marked by generosity, gratitude, and a relentless pursuit of Your Divine Will. In Jesus' Name I pray, Amen.

PRAYER OVERRIDE 18

The Mark of Deafness

Heavenly Father, I come before You with a humble heart, recognizing that You are the Giver of every good and perfect gift. Lord, I thank You for blessing me not only with natural senses but also with Spiritual Senses designed to draw me nearer to You. I acknowledge that *The Mark of Deafness* is not simply a physical inability to hear, but a Spiritual Condition that can cloud my discernment, hinder my obedience, and distance me from Your Divine Presence. I ask for Your mercy and forgiveness for every time I have ignored or resisted Your Voice, whether out of fear, pride, or distraction.

Holy Spirit, search me and reveal every area where I have grown dull to Your promptings. Shine Your light on the hidden places in my soul where I have closed my ears to Your commands and guidance. I confess that there are moments when I have chosen comfort over conviction, and convenience over commitment. Lord, forgive me for treating Your precious gifts with carelessness, for discarding the tools and treasures You have placed in my life, especially when trials or disappointments have tempted me to give up.

Father, I am reminded by Your Word that it is possible to see and not perceive, to hear and not understand. I do not want to be among those who walk blindly through life, missing the richness of Your Spirit and the depth of Your Divine Wisdom. Open my Spiritual ears, Lord, so that I may hear You clearly. Remove every barrier of disobedience, lukewarmness, and stubbornness that prevents me from receiving Your instructions. I desire to honor and cherish the Spiritual Gifts You have given me, using them faithfully for Your glory and the advancement of Your Kingdom.

When I am tempted to throw away what You have entrusted to me out of frustration or weariness, remind me of the value You see in me and in the Spiritual Gifts You have lovingly bestowed within me. Help me to persevere in developing my Spiritual Senses, even when the journey is difficult. Let me not fall into the enemy's trap of Spiritual Disconnection, nor allow disappointment to breed indifference or irrelevance within me. Teach me to seek Your face with diligence, *Spirit to Spirit*, until every blockage is removed and my heart is fully attuned to Your Heavenly Voice.

Lord, I ask that You would guard me against the subtle ways the enemy exploits deafness in my life. Protect me from the dangers of self-will, pride, and rebellion. Make me sensitive to Your correction and eager for Your guidance. Help me to lay aside every hindrance, every distraction, and every stubborn habit that keeps me from walking in sync with Your Spirit.

Father, I pray for the courage to obey You, even when I do not fully understand, and the faith to trust You, even when Your instructions challenge my comfort. Let every Spiritual Gift, Tool, and Principle You have given me find its fullest expression in my life. May I never take for granted the Kingdom Treasures You have placed in my hands, or the usage of them.

Lord, renew my mind and soften my heart so that I may be quick to listen, slow to speak, and eager to do Your Divine Will. Help me not to squander my Spiritual Inheritance, nor to allow my legacy, my seed, or my purpose to suffer because of my negligence. Let my life be a TESTIMONY of a heart that hears, a Spirit that responds, and a soul that is fully surrendered to You.

Holy Spirit, unclog my ears and attune my heart to Your frequency. Teach me to recognize Your Supernatural Whispers, heed Your Spiritual Warnings, and follow Your Divine Directions with delightfulness and gratitude. Restore to me the joy of hearing Your Heavenly Voice and walking in OBEDIENCE to Your Word.

Father, I thank You for Your Supernatural Patience and for the second chances You grant me to get it right. May I rise above every *Mark of Deafness* and step boldly into my Divine Destiny as a faithful listener, an obedient servant, and as a conduit in Earthen Vessel for Your glory. In Jesus' Name I pray, Amen.

PRAYER OVERRIDE 19

The Mark of Delusion

Heavenly Father, I approach Your throne with awe and humility, recognizing that I am in Earthen Vessel in need of Your truth and Your light. Lord, I confess that in my journey through life, I have often struggled with the battle between truth and deception. I acknowledge that *The Mark of Delusion* is a real and present danger, seeking to ensnare my Mind, Body, Soul, and Spirit, sometimes without me even realizing it. I admit that delusion has a way of finding me, testing my faith, my discernment, and my allegiance to You. However, I will not relent to it, as You are the Author and Finisher of my faith.

Father, I ask for Your Divine Protection and Supernatural Wisdom as I navigate the complexities of this world. When confusion or false beliefs try to take hold, remind me to suit up with the Whole Armor of God, as You command. Help me to fasten the Belt of Truth around my waist, so that deception finds no entry point in my life. Let the Breastplate of Righteousness guard my heart, so that I may stand blameless before You. Allow the Shoes of the Gospel of Peace to guide my steps, so I may walk in confidence and not fear. Strengthen my grip on the Shield of Faith, so that every fiery dart of the enemy is extinguished before it can harm me. Place firmly upon my head the Helmet of Salvation, so my thoughts remain anchored in Your Divine Promises. Grant me a steady hand with the Sword of the Spirit, which is Your Word, keeping me sharp, alert, and ready to contend for the faith You have given me.

Holy Spirit, I invite You to illuminate every hidden area of delusion in my life. Reveal to me where I have believed lies, followed after my own feelings, or operated in confusion rather than in faith. Cleanse me of every false narrative that has polluted my mind or dulled my discernment. Restore my Spirit to clarity, so that I may remain in true *Spirit to Spirit* connection with You. When static interference clouds my understanding, break through the noise with the thunderous truth of Your Holy Presence. Remind me that my feelings are not my faith, and that my hope must always rest in You.

Lord, I repent for every moment I have given in to self-pleasure, despair, or the temptation to give up. Strengthen me so that I never bow to the pressures of the adversary. Grant me the WISDOM of Proverbs, so that my mouth and my actions reflect Your Divine Knowledge and not the folly of the world. Let me not store up words of destruction, but rather, fill my heart and mind with Your Heavenly Wisdom and Treasures, that I may be a storehouse for Your Kingdom.

Father, help me to recognize that living according to Your Divine Will does not guarantee ease, but it does grant understanding. Teach me to value understanding above comfort, so that I may not perish from the lack of knowledge. Let my life be a TESTAMENT to the pursuit of truth, even when it requires me to work, repent, and continually seek Your Divine Guidance, just as King David did. Let me never be so proud or stubborn that I reject the knowledge You offer, or forget the Spiritual Principles and Laws You have written upon my heart.

Holy Spirit, give me discernment to recognize the subtle tactics of the enemy and the courage to address them head-on. Help me to guard my Spirit from delusion by meditating on Your Word, spending time in prayer, and remaining vigilant in faith. Show me how to suit up daily, not just for my own sake, but for the sake of all those connected to me, especially the innocent children who depend on my Spiritual Clarity and Strength.

Lord, I ask that You keep me from the trap of pretending the adversary does not exist. Sharpen my awareness to the reality of Spiritual Warfare and empower me to stand strong in Your might. When I falter or become weary, renew my resolve to seek You, to trust You, and to live in a way that PLEASES You.

Father, I lay every false belief, every misunderstanding, and every deceptive influence at Your feet. Replace them with truth, clarity, and unwavering faith. Let my life be marked by discernment, wisdom, and the unshakable assurance that comes from knowing and loving You. In Jesus' Name I pray, Amen.

PRAYER OVERRIDE 20

The Mark of Denial

Heavenly Father, I come before You, grateful for Your Divine Presence and Your unwavering truth. In Earthen Vessel, shaped by Your hands, only You truly sees the depths of my heart and the invisible marks that define my life. Lord, I confess that at times, I have allowed *The Mark of Denial* to shape how I see myself, how others see me, and how I believe You see me. I have cared about people, places, and things that do not truly matter, often neglecting what is most important to You.

Father, I ask You to open my mind and heart to the truths that I have ignored or denied. Reveal to me the subtle ways denial has crept into my thoughts, choices, and relationships. Show me where I have fixed what was never broken or broken what only You can repair. Help me to distinguish between the truths I accept and the ones I have avoided, the doubts I endure and the ones I reject. Let my life be marked by honesty and courage, rather than self-deception or avoidance.

Holy Spirit, search every corner of my being. Expose the hidden forces and character traits that keep me in denial, whether it is arrogance, disobedience, dullness, or emotional unintelligence. Uncover the places where I have created Spiritual Taboos or Yokes through the use of my own words, desires, attitudes, reactions, and actions. Guard me from becoming the enemy's laughingstock, thinking I am strong when I am actually weak in denial, blaming others for my own shortcomings, or giving the adversary access to sift me through my lack of self-awareness.

Lord, I realize that to walk in Divine Intelligence, I must regulate my emotions and respond to others with kindness, empathy, respect, and sincerity. Teach me to put my psyche in check so that my selfish wants and desires do not contaminate my Spirit or disqualify me. Show me how to Spiritually Till my own ground, using the Fruits of the Spirit and living Christlike. Do not let me become a toxic cesspool of negativity, overflowing into the lives of others and distancing me from the living water You intend for me.

Father, help me to take responsibility for my emotional and Spiritual Well-Being. Remind me that I must do the necessary work to keep the adversary from gaining leverage over my Mind, Body, Soul, and Spirit. Let me not expect others to do for me what You have called me to do for myself. Grant me Divine and Emotional Intelligence so that I may develop self-awareness, self-regulation, and self-correction in line with Your Divine Will. May I never become so heavenly-minded that I am of no earthly good.

Holy Spirit, help me recognize the difference between what is right and wrong, positive and negative, just and unjust. Uproot any Spiritual Blindness, Deafness, or Muteness within me. If I have ever traumatized Your sheep or failed to offer life-giving wisdom, forgive me and grant me the humility to learn and grow. Let me never indulge in foolery, constant complaints, or compromise Your Word. Shield me from giving my enemies leverage over me by remaining in denial or refusing to take responsibility for every aspect of my being.

Lord, when I am broken to the core or struggling to fight back, let Your Divine Intervention meet me in my weakness. Draw me back to the Source of all strength. Cover me with the Blood of Jesus. Invigorate my Spirit with the power of the Holy Spirit. Awaken me from any slumber, disappointment, or Spiritual Stagnation. Let me thirst for the living water that springs up into everlasting life, cleansing every cesspool of negativity and transforming it into a stream of grace, love, mercy, and hope.

Father, I surrender my denial, my pride, and my frailty to You. I ask for the courage to face the truth, the wisdom to accept it, and the humility to change. Restore me, renew me, and let my life bear witness to the power of honest self-examination and Divine Transformation. In Jesus' Name I pray, Amen.

PRAYER OVERRIDE 21

The Mark of Disappointment

Heavenly Father, I come before You with a tender and searching heart, recognizing that disappointment is a part of my journey on this earth. Lord, I confess that there have been moments when disappointments have lingered in my mind, leaving marks on my soul that shape the way I think, act, and dream. Sometimes the sting of unmet expectations, failures, and losses has felt overwhelming. I acknowledge that these marks are not just fleeting emotions, but Divine Invitations to look deeper into myself, to seek Your Divine Wisdom, and to grow in faith and resilience.

Father, I thank You for the lessons embedded in every disappointment. I ask for the courage to question what I thought I knew about failure and to see each letdown as an opportunity for transformation. When I am faced with setbacks, help me to resist the urge to wallow in regret or to settle in dry places. Instead, empower me to rise up, to speak life into my dry bones, and to pursue restoration along with my Blueprinted Purpose with boldness and tenacity, as You have shown throughout Your Word.

Lord, I realize that disappointment often comes when my expectations do not align with reality, whether real or imagined. When I am tempted to lose my footing, remind me that my VALUE and my power are rooted in You, not in the opinions or actions of others. Help me to shake off discouragement, regroup, and move forward in the Spirit of Excellence. Where I have struggled to understand the reasons for my pain, give me clarity, understanding, and the patience to endure.

Holy Spirit, search my heart and reveal any place where disappointment has taken root as bitterness, hopelessness, or fear. Remove every yoke, soul tie, or oppression that tries to keep me captive, trapped, or traumatized. If I have placed value in things or people who do not prioritize You or me, teach me how to redirect my focus, *As It Pleases You.* Help me to establish the true value of coming into Divine Alignment with Your Kingdom. Grant me the

Supernatural Wisdom to discern what is HOLY and what is not to protect me from casting my pearls before swine.

Father, I ask for the grace to see the solution that may already be within my grasp or deep within my soul. When I forget who I am as Your child, remind me that I am the Temple of the Holy Spirit, a Sacred Space in which Your Spirit dwells. Please, My Lord, do not allow disappointment to cause me to forfeit my identity or the Divine Greatness You have placed inside of me. Help me to participate in my own restoration, partnering with You to walk boldly in my Predetermined Purpose and to protect the Spiritual Gifts You have entrusted me with.

Lord, I thank You for the strength to stand tall with my scars and all. For I know beyond a shadow of a doubt that my healing comes through repentance, forgiveness, prayer, fasting, and trusting You beyond what I see, hear, or experience. For this reason, I speak life into every dry valley and to each dry bone, asking for Supernatural Discernment and Wisdom beyond human understanding, as I navigate through my known and unknown challenges.

Holy Spirit, develop within me Spiritual Discernment so that I may recognize, interpret, and respond to Your guidance with sincerity and humility. Help me to differentiate truth from falsehood, good from evil, and to always align my life with Your Divine Will. Amid all, I cover myself with the Blood of Jesus, invite the Holy Spirit into every situation, bear the Fruits of the Spirit, and walk in Christlike character.

Father, I surrender all my disappointments, unmet expectations, and heartaches to You. Transform *The Mark of Disappointment* into a TESTIMONY of Your faithfulness and grace. As my life becomes marked by hope, resilience, wisdom, and unwavering trust in You, equip me to overcome every challenge to shine bright like a DIAMOND. In Jesus' Name I pray, Amen.

PRAYER OVERRIDE 22

The Mark of Disobedience

Heavenly Father, I come before You with a heart that longs to PLEASE You and to walk in Divine Alignment with Your perfect will. Lord, I confess that *The Mark of Disobedience* has sometimes found a nesting place within me, whether in my thoughts, words, actions, motives, or subtle choices that escape the notice of others. Therefore, I repent for allowing a negative nest as such to fester. I acknowledge that nothing comes into reality without first taking root within my heart. I ask for Your forgiveness for every hidden act, every unaddressed attitude, and every moment I have chosen my own way over Yours.

Father, I recognize that true purity and righteousness are not found in outward appearances, but in the honesty and humility of my inner life. I admit that I am far from being clean as a whistle, and that pride, resentment, fear, and self-deception can find their way into my soul. Thank You for the gifts of repentance, mercy, compassion, and forgiveness that offer me a path to restoration and healing. Lord, protect me from the subtle lies I tell myself, and expose every area where I have been dishonest, defensive, judgmental, or unwilling to admit my faults. Let me not be blinded by self-importance, but instead, clothe me in meekness and genuine self-awareness.

Holy Spirit, reveal to me the root causes or seeds of my disobedience and the patterns of thought, belief, and behavior that keep me bound. Break the cycle of repeating my own mistakes, and help me to recognize, document, and surrender every unrighteous inclination. Give me the courage to demand my freedom based on Your Word, to repent and forgive as needed, and to surrender to Your correction. As I cover my weaknesses, failures, and struggles with the Blood of Jesus, I invite the Holy Spirit to move powerfully within me, guiding, convicting, and transforming me from the inside out.

Lord, I thank You that You have not left me helpless or defenseless in this struggle. You have equipped me with the Whole Armor of God, Divine

Provisions, the guidance of the Holy Spirit, and the assurance of victory through Christ Jesus. Help me to use these Spiritual Tools not for my benefit alone, but as a TESTIMONY to Your faithfulness and power. Let me not merely recite Your Word, but live it, apply it, and share it through my actions, reactions, thoughts, words, and beliefs, always seeking to reflect Christlike character.

Father, I ask for the discernment to recognize when I am blaming others, rationalizing, minimizing sin, or making excuses for my actions. Keep me from Spiritualizing my disobedience, delaying repentance, or redefining right and wrong to fit my preferences. Let me not seek the approval of others over Your approval, nor use outward conformity or religious rituals to mask what is truly in my heart. Deliver me from denial, self-pity, and the temptation to blame the enemy for my own choices. Instead, grant me the grace to accept responsibility, to embrace true repentance, and to walk in authentic obedience.

Holy Spirit, open my Spiritual Eyes, ears, and intellect so that I may receive Divine Downloads, *Spirit to Spirit*, and operate with accuracy, intentionality, and reverence in all that I do. Help me to master the art of self-correction, continually training my thoughts, emotions, and actions to align with Your Divine Will. Let my life be a stream of living water, not a cesspool of negativity or deception, and may my TESTIMONY shine as a beacon of hope, love, and unity.

Lord, I desire to be counted among the faithful, vigilant, and devoted. Guard me from the deceptive marks of the enemy and seal me with the Spiritual Seal of the Living God. Teach me to value Your guidance above all else, to live with a knowing and a willingness to do what PLEASES You, and to walk in the fullness of my Divine Purpose. May I never abuse the anointing You have placed upon my life, but use it to glorify You, serve others, and advance Your Kingdom with excellence and integrity.

Father, I surrender every area of disobedience to You. Cleanse me, restore me, and empower me to live victoriously. Let my life be marked not by rebellion, but by unwavering obedience, hope, and love. In Jesus' Name I pray, Amen.

PRAYER OVERRIDE 23

The Mark of Disrespectfulness

Heavenly Father, I come before You with a humble and searching heart, acknowledging that *The Mark of Disrespectfulness* is a force that can subtly invade my thoughts, words, and actions. Lord, I confess that at times I have allowed disrespect, whether intentional or unintentional, to shape my relationships, my perspective, and my servanthood. I recognize that acts of disregard, judgment, or discrimination, no matter how small, can leave lasting impressions on others and on my soul.

Father, I ask You to open my eyes to every area where I have failed to honor those around me. Forgive me for moments when I have allowed my own insecurities, biases, or frustrations to foster disrespect toward my elders, my peers, strangers, or even myself. Cleanse my heart of every trace of Spiritual Discrimination, pride, or false sense of values that would cause me to look down on others or to judge what I cannot see. Remove from me any tendency to dismiss, diminish, or devalue anyone You have created.

Holy Spirit, shine Your light on the hidden prejudices, the silent judgments, and the subtle discriminations that reside in me. Help me to recognize the humanity and dignity in every person, regardless of their abilities, differences, background, or status. I repent for any way that I have contributed to division, chaos, or the erosion of unity in my home, my community, or the Body of Christ. Instill within me a Spirit of Empathy, Humility, and Love that transcends my limitations.

Lord, I know that everyone carries battles, burdens, or weaknesses, some visible, some hidden. Let me not lie to myself about my own vulnerabilities, nor use them as weapons against others. Teach me to extend the same mercy to others that I desperately need for myself. I am reminded that I may be entertaining Angels unaware, and that I do not have the right to judge or condemn anyone. Only You truly know the hearts and motives of Your children.

Father, give me the strength to stand for unity, to heal wounds where I can, and to be a conduit of Your peace. When I am tempted to discriminate, ridicule, or exclude, remind me of Abraham's plea for mercy and his resolve to preserve a legacy of compassion and forgiveness. Grant me the wisdom to see beyond the surface, to value my people skills and Christlike Character Traits above status, fame, or wealth.

Holy Spirit, uproot every generational curse, every pattern of disrespect, and every barrier to unity that may exist within my family or me. Help me to become an agent of reconciliation, restoring trust, dignity, and hope wherever I go. Let me be quick to extend grace, slow to judge, and eager to honor others in word and deed.

Lord, I surrender my need to be right, my fears of being different, and my pride that erects walls instead of bridges. Fill me with Your Spirit so that I may love as You love, serve as You serve, and see as You see. Use my life to bring healing to those wounded by disrespect, and to be a shining example of the unity, mercy, and respect that You desire for all Your children.

Father, I invite You to search me and know me. Cleanse me of every *Mark of Disrespectfulness* and transform my heart to reflect Your Divine Love and Compassion. May my words, actions, thoughts, and attitudes bring GLORY to the Kingdom and MULTIPLYING BLESSING to those around me. In Jesus' Name I pray, Amen.

PRAYER OVERRIDE 24

The Mark of Dissatisfaction

Heavenly Father, I come before You with an open and reflective heart, fully aware that *The Mark of Dissatisfaction* has lingered in my life, sometimes hidden in plain sight and sometimes masked by denial, avoidance, or self-centeredness. Lord, I confess that there have been moments when I have pacified uncomfortable truths, resisted learning from the past, or refused to confront the realities that shape my present and future. I recognize that this pattern of avoidance does not please You, and it keeps me from the deeper wisdom, discernment, and peace that You desire for me.

Father, I ask You to cleanse my heart from every root of dissatisfaction. Reveal to me the places where I have accepted cycles of ignorance, repeated mistakes, or generational secrets without questioning or seeking Your truth. Help me to approach information, history, and even my own shortcomings with humility, a willingness to learn, and a posture that seeks Your Divine Guidance above all. Teach me to eat the MEAT of Your Word and spit out the bones, discerning what is true, valuable, and necessary for my growth, and releasing what does not serve my Spirit.

Holy Spirit, search me and know me. Remove every proud look, lying tongue, or deceitful posture from my life. Cleanse my hands, my heart, my thoughts, and my words from anything that sows discord, devises wicked plans, or runs swiftly to evil. If I have ever secured family secrets, hidden dysfunction, or perpetuated cycles of avoidance, I repent and ask for Your healing in my family line. Break every generational curse and every cycle of secrecy that keeps me, my loved ones, or my community from true freedom.

Lord, I desire to PLEASE You above all else. Give me the humility to admit my shortcomings and the courage to address the issues that cause restlessness, confusion, or unease in my soul. Let me not be satisfied with superficial peace or fleeting pleasures, but instead, grant me the hunger for lasting transformation, true wisdom, and Spiritual Maturity. Help me to

TEST the Spirit and the fruit of my life, aligning myself with Your Word and gleaning the lessons You present to me, even when they are difficult to face.

Father, I surrender every area of dissatisfaction to You, whether it is with myself, with others, or with You. Heal my heart, renew my mind, and grant me a *Spirit to Spirit* connection that cannot be shaken by the storms of life or the shadows of the past. Let my home, my community, my workplace, and my church be places where honesty, humility, and Divine Wisdom reign, breaking through every stronghold of secrecy, shame, or dysfunction.

Holy Spirit, empower me to approach life with a work-in-progress mindset, always open to Divine Correction, always eager for deeper understanding, and always ready for the freedom that comes with Your truth. May *The Mark of Dissatisfaction* be erased from my life, replaced by contentment, gratitude, discernment, and a relentless pursuit of all that PLEASES You.

Father, I thank You for the PROMISE that what is hidden will be revealed, and what is broken can be restored. I trust in Your Divine timing, Your Supernatural Wisdom, and Your Everlasting Love as I walk forward, leaving behind the cycles of dissatisfaction and embracing the fullness of Your Predestined Blueprinted Plan for me. In Jesus' Name I pray, Amen.

Dr. Y. Bur

www.DrYBur.com

PRAYER OVERRIDE 25

The Mark of Distrust

Heavenly Father, I come before You with a heart that seeks truth and restoration, fully aware that *The Mark of Distrust* has clouded my *Spirit to Spirit* relationship with You, with others, and even with myself. Lord, I confess that I have sometimes allowed doubt, suspicion, or fear to shape my perceptions, my reactions, and my interactions. I acknowledge that trust is the cornerstone of my Spiritual Life, and that without it, my foundation is shaky and my vision is obscured.

Father, I ask You to examine every area of my life where distrust has taken root. Reveal to me the wounds, disappointments, betrayals, traumas, or misunderstandings that have distorted my ability to trust. If I have unknowingly doubted Your goodness, Your timing, or Your faithfulness, forgive me and renew my Spirit, allowing me to trust You in all things, even when I do not understand Your ways. If I have doubted myself or the intentions of others, heal me and grant me discernment to distinguish truth from deception, wisdom from folly, and right from wrong.

Holy Spirit, teach me to surrender my need for control, my fears of being disappointed, and my tendency to hold back my trust. Show me how to let go of the illusion of control and to embrace the vulnerabilities that come with exuding genuine faith. Help me to trust in the unseen, to believe in Your purpose even when the outcome is hidden, and to rest in Your promises when circumstances shake my confidence.

Lord, I recognize that distrust can be contagious, spreading through families, friendships, and communities, undermining the very bonds that hold us together. Where I have contributed to division, suspicion, or the erosion of trust, forgive me and empower me to be an agent of reconciliation. Let my words, thoughts, and actions consistently reflect the Fruits of the Spirit, building bridges of integrity, honesty, and unconditional love.

Father, where I have been a conditional giver, offering love, support, or generosity with strings attached, cleanse my motives and teach me to give selflessly. Help me to love without expectation, serve without manipulation, and relate to others with the same grace and freedom You have extended to me. If I have been the recipient of conditional giving or manipulation, grant me the wisdom to set healthy boundaries and the strength to walk in truth and freedom.

Holy Spirit, renew my mind and transform my heart so that the renewing of my mind may continually transform me, as Your Word instructs my every footstep, *As It Pleases You*. Remove every root of distrust, pride, or bitterness, and fill me with unwavering faith, hope, and love. Let me be quick to listen, slow to speak, and even slower to judge, eagerly believing the best in others, while always seeking unity and peace.

Lord, I invite You to search me and know me. Heal every wound, restore every broken place, and remove every *Mark of Distrust* from my life. Let my relationships be built on a foundation of trust, transparency, and mutual respect, reflecting the love and faithfulness that are found in You alone.

Father, I choose to trust You wholeheartedly and *Spirit to Spirit*. I choose to trust the Great Works You are doing in me in Earthen Vessel. And, most of all, my Lord, for my Heaven on Earth Experience, I also choose to trust that Your Divine Plans for me are for the Greater Good of all mankind, *As It Pleases You*. May *The Mark of Distrust* be replaced with the Divine Seal of Your Spirit, anchoring me in faith and empowering me to live with confidence and peace. In Jesus' Name I pray, Amen.

PRAYER OVERRIDE 26

The Mark of Division

Heavenly Father, I come before You in humility and reverence, acknowledging that *The Mark of Division* is a force that seeks to separate, to fracture, and to undermine the unity You desire for all of us, Your children. Lord, I confess that at times, I have allowed divided thoughts, doubts, and uncertainties to take root in my mind. I recognize that when my thoughts are scattered as my loyalties become divided and unpleasing to You, I become unstable, wavering, and confused. Lord, when in this state, I am unable to make sound decisions or to honor You with my whole heart; therefore, I seek to correct this matter in the Name of Jesus.

Father, I ask You to shine Your light on every area of my life where division has been allowed to grow, whether in my relationships, my home, my community, my church, or my nation. If I have been complicit in sowing seeds of discord, mistrust, or disharmony, forgive me and cleanse my heart from every root of bitterness or resentment. Help me to recognize the subtle ways that division disguises itself through gossip, pride, unforgiveness, and competing agendas. Show me how my words, actions, or even my silent thoughts may have contributed to division instead of unity.

Holy Spirit, search me and reveal every place where I have entertained double-mindedness or wishy-washy thinking. Grant me the courage to confront my own doubts and fears, and to surrender them to You. Teach me to stand firm in faith, to choose unity over strife, and to seek reconciliation over retaliation. Show me where I have allowed the serpent of doubt to plant seeds in my heart, where I have questioned Your Word, Your goodness, or the worth of others. Uproot those seeds and replace them with unwavering trust and love.

Lord, I desire to be an agent of unity, a builder of bridges, and a peacemaker in every sphere You have placed me. Let my mind be renewed and my thoughts aligned with Your truth. Grant me the Divine Wisdom to discern the dividing lines between healthy boundaries and harmful walls. Help me to recognize when division is present, not so I may cast blame, but so I may respond with humility and grace, seeking restoration and healing above all else.

Father, I pray for every relationship that has been marked by division, whether through misunderstanding, betrayal, or differing perspectives. Heal what has been broken, restore what has been lost, and bring forth Your Spirit of reconciliation, *As It Pleases You*. Let forgiveness flow freely, and let pride, envy, and judgment give way to kindness and understanding.

Holy Spirit, empower me to overcome every *Mark of Division* within myself. Where I am at war within my very own psyche, bring me peace. Where I am pulled in many directions, center me in Your Divine Will. Where I have lost sight of my purpose, restore my focus and clarity. May my life reflect the unity of the Spirit and the bond of peace, that I may be known as a child of God who chooses unity over discord.

Lord, I ask that You would protect my heart, my mind, and my relationships from the schemes of the enemy. Guard me against the temptation to divide, to take sides, or to isolate myself from those You have called me to love. Let me be quick to offer a listening ear, a well-governed tongue that speaks life, and eager to understand You, myself, and others, *As It Pleases You*. Fill me with compassion, wisdom, and the desire to pursue harmony in all things.

Father, may the *Mark of Division* be expunged from my life, replaced by the Divine Seal of Your Spirit, the power of Your love, and the beauty of true unity. Let my words and deeds be a TESTIMONY to Your reconciling grace and mercy. Unite my heart in ONENESS with You and to live as one who brings people together under the banner of Christ. In Jesus' Name I pray, Amen.

PRAYER OVERRIDE 27

The Mark of Dominance

Heavenly Father, I come before You with reverence and humility, acknowledging that *The Mark of Dominance* has shaped my thoughts, actions, and relationships in ways that I may not always see. Lord, I confess that there have been moments when I have sought to control, to assert my own will, or to pursue power for the sake of my ego rather than for Your glory. I realize that true worth and purpose come not from dominating others, but from walking in unity, humility, and according to the Divine Calling You have placed upon my life.

Father, I ask that You examine my motives and purify my heart. Reveal to me every area where I have operated out of self-interest, pride, or a desire to control. Teach me the difference between Divine Dominion and worldly dominance, so that I may lead and influence others in a way that reflects Your Spirit and Your love. Let my confidence, vision, and determination be rooted in Your Divine Will, not in a need to prove myself or to become a demigod over others.

Holy Spirit, fill me with self-control, kindness, gentleness, humility, and patience. Empower me to use my Spiritual Gifts and Divine Authority not to manipulate or overpower, but to serve, encourage, and uplift those around me. Give me the wisdom to know when to speak, when to be silent, when to take action, and when to step back. Help me to lead by example, always pointing others to Christ by the way I live, love, and forgive.

Lord, I recognize that true greatness is found in servanthood, and that Your Kingdom is advanced not by force, but by love, mercy, and a Spirit of Unity. Help me to let go of the need to change others and to focus on cultivating my own character and obedience to You. Remind me that my power is best reserved for the battles that matter, the battles for justice, for truth, for peace, and for the well-being of others.

Father, I surrender the areas of my life where dominance has taken root. I release every desire to be right, to be first, or to have my way. Instead, I choose to walk worthy of the calling with which I have been called, with all humility, gentleness, and longsuffering, bearing with others in love, and endeavoring to keep the UNITY of the Spirit with a bond of peace. Guide me to till the garden of my heart, cultivating purity, dedication, and Spiritual Devotion as You intended from the beginning.

Holy Spirit, help me to recognize the Divine Blessings already within my reach. Remove my Spiritual Blinders, untie every soul tie, and silence every dream killer that would keep me from seeing and embracing Your Spiritual Gifts. Grant me the discernment to let go of what is not mine to control and the gratitude to celebrate the blessings I have. Let contentment, gratitude, and peace reign in my heart, home, and relationships.

Lord, I ask that You heal any wounds I have caused by my dominance or control. Restore unity where there has been division, and bring reconciliation where there has been strife. Let my legacy be one of building others up, not tearing them down. May I always choose the path of love, humility, and Christlike character.

Father, I thank You for the Divine Light and Supernatural Wisdom You have placed within me. I commit to nurturing them, *As It Pleases You*. I am also dedicated to walking in my Predestined Blueprinted Purpose, and to honor You in all that I do, say, and become. May *The Mark of Dominance* be replaced by the SEAL of Your Spirit, and may my life be a Testimony of Servant Leadership, Godly Unity, and Divine Love. In Jesus' Name I pray, Amen.

PRAYER OVERRIDE 28

The Mark of Doubt

Heavenly Father, I come before You with a humble and open heart, asking for Your guidance as I reflect upon *The Mark of Doubt*. I acknowledge that doubt is a path every human must tread, a shadow that visits each of us, sometimes silently and other times with overwhelming force. I confess, Lord, that I have experienced this mark in moments of uncertainty, when I have questioned my worth, my abilities, my readiness, and even Your Divine Promises over my life. Even in solitude, when no one is watching, doubt can chip away at my confidence and distort the truth about who I am in You.

Yet, Father, I thank You for the dual nature of doubt, for it can serve as a signal to seek deeper understanding, to ask profound questions, and to grow in wisdom. I recognize that it is not doubt itself, but my response to it, that shapes my destiny. Your Word shows me that even the faithful have wrestled with doubt, but You remain patient, steadfast, and loving as we find our way back to assurance in You.

Lord, I ask You to search my thoughts and expose any hidden places where doubt has settled. Illuminate those corners of my mind and heart that have become playgrounds for the enemy, where unresolved trauma or fear has fanned the flames of insecurity. I surrender those places to You, trusting that Your Spirit will uproot every seed of doubt and replace it with faith, hope, understanding, and clarity.

I pray for the wisdom to use doubt as a stepping stone rather than a stumbling block. Help me to see every hesitation as an opportunity to prepare more diligently, to trust Your timing, and to rely on Your strength instead of my own. Let doubt inspire me to seek, to learn, to stretch beyond my comfort zones, and to pursue the fullness of the potential You have placed within me.

Father, I repent for the times I have allowed doubt to lead me away from Your Divine Will, causing me to settle for less or abandon the dreams You have instilled in my heart. Forgive me for the moments I have downplayed my readiness or underestimated the Spiritual Gifts You have given me. With Your help, I choose to reverse every negative thought, every false projection, and every mark of the enemy by aligning my mind with Your truth. I declare that I will override *The Mark of Doubt* with the mark of faith, courage, and perseverance, *As It Pleases You.*

Gracious God, I recognize that idolatrous thinking can subtly weave its way into my mind, causing me to depend on people, possessions, or status rather than on You, the True Source. I ask that You open my Spiritual Eyes to see as You see, my Spiritual Ears to hear Your Divine Wisdom, and my mouth to speak words that build up, encourage, and glorify You, *As It Pleases You.* Reveal to me any patterns of thinking that have become idols in my life, and empower me to dismantle them through the renewing of my mind.

Lord, help me to engage in corrective thinking by reversing every unjust, unrighteous, or self-limiting belief. Teach me to embrace the fullness of the thinking styles You have GIFTED me with. Be it critical, creative, analytical, reflective, practical, systems, divergent, convergent, abstract, quantitative, and concrete, they are mine to use, *As It Pleases You,* so that I may approach life's challenges with a sound mind, a steadfast Spirit, and a heart anchored in Your truth.

Today, I ask for Divine Guidance in every decision, every relationship, and every season of growth. Let Your Divine Light dispel the darkness of doubt so that I may walk boldly in my calling, free from the shackles of insecurity and fear. May my thoughts, words, and actions be PLEASING in Your sight and serve the Greater Good of all mankind.

Thank You for Your unwavering love, for the power to overcome, and for the PROMISE that when I seek You, I will find You, *Spirit to Spirit.* Strengthen me daily to choose faith over doubt, certainty over uncertainty, and Your Divine Will over my own. In Jesus' Name I pray, Amen.

PRAYER OVERRIDE 29

The Mark of Dullness

Heavenly Father, I come before You in humility and reverence, seeking Your Divine Wisdom and Everlasting Grace as I reflect on *The Mark of Dullness*. Lord, I acknowledge that Spiritual Dullness can settle into my heart and mind in subtle ways, drawing me away from Your Heavenly Presence, muting my discernment, and making me unresponsive to Your Divine Voice. I ask You to search the depths and corners of my psyche and reveal any area where dullness has taken root, whether through complacency, sorrow, trauma, conditioning, or neglect.

Father, I confess that there have been times when my heart has grown wearily insensitive, my ears have struggled to hear Your Sacred Whispers, and my eyes have closed to Your wonders. In these moments, I have missed opportunities for growth, healing, and a deeper intimacy with You, *Spirit to Spirit*. Thus, I repent as I formally ask for healing, restoration, and understanding. *As It Pleases You.*

Lord, as I seek to override *The Mark of Dullness* in my life, I pray for the courage to face myself honestly. Please help me to take accountability for my actions, words, thoughts, beliefs, or desires as I pursue continual transformation, *As It Pleases You*. In addition, assist me in recognizing when I have become stagnant, unmotivated, or resistant to change. Remind me that dullness is not a permanent sentence or state of being, but a season that Your Spirit can redeem me for the Greater Good.

My God, You have placed within me a Genius that is rooted in my Spiritual Heritaged DNA. Let me not deny the Spiritual Gifts, Calling, or Purpose You have Divinely Woven into my being. Help me to embrace my Genetic and Spiritual Makeup, to own my truth, and to bring my unique contribution to the unity and benefit of Your precious sheep. Where there is imbalance, strife, or envy, fill me with Your Holy Spirit and cover me with the Blood of Jesus, so I may walk in genuineness, kindness, and self-control, *As It Pleases You.*

Father, I recognize that my words hold great power. Guard the gateway of my mouth, so that my speech may edify, restore, heal, empower, and bring grace to others from the least to the greatest. Give me Supernatural Wisdom to bridle my tongue, to speak with respect and love, and to refrain from words that sow discord or destruction. When I am tempted to respond without thinking or allow my tone to wound myself or others, convict me gently and redirect my heart and mind posture toward righteousness.

Holy Spirit, renew my mind and SHARPEN my discernment faculties, so I may not grieve You with my careless words, thoughts, desires, or actions. Teach me to listen carefully, to seek understanding, and to offer forgiveness as freely as You have forgiven me. Help me to cultivate a tender heart, filled with compassion and humility, that reflects Your Divine Love and Mercy to all I encounter on my Spiritual Journey.

Lord, I pray that I will never use the excuse of dullness or lack of self-control to justify my shortcomings or hinder the Spiritual Gifts You have entrusted to me. Strengthen my resolve to honor You in all I do and say, and to strive for excellence as I grow in average wisdom and maturity, graduating to the Divine Status of them. Let me recognize and dismantle any patterns of behavior that block my Genius from Within, so Your Divine Light may shine brightly through me with the Spiritual Illumination from the Heavenly of Heavens.

Thank You for Your continual guidance as I seek the Divine Sharpening needed through Your Spirit, one to another. My Lord, as I find clarity, purpose, and success, going from average or normal to Supernatural or Divine, grant me the discipline to prepare diligently, the humility to learn from my mistakes, and the resilience to rise above my secret or open lethargy and distractions. As I awaken from my slumber, may my life be a LIVING TESTIMONY to Your transforming power and boundless grace.

My Heavenly Father, I trust in Your faithfulness to restore what has grown dull, to revive what has faded, and to renew what has been neglected. I surrender my heart, my mind, my words, my thoughts, my desires, my habits, my actions, and my everything to You. *Spirit to Spirit*, my Lord, I am asking for a fresh OUTPOURING of Your Spirit so I may walk in Divine Wisdom, Unity, and Love, *As It Pleases You*, superseding the average or the basic to become Spiritually Sharp. In Jesus' Name I pray, Amen.

PRAYER OVERRIDE 30

The Mark of Envy and Jealousy

Heavenly Father, I come before You with an open heart, honestly acknowledging the presence and influence of envy and jealousy in my life. I thank You for the wisdom to see these emotions not as marks of shame, but as invitations to a deeper self-examination and growth in Earthen Vessel. Lord, I recognize that these feelings are signals pointing to my unmet needs, old wounds, unresolved traumas, or fears that I may not have fully addressed. I ask for Your Divine Guidance, Mercy, and Grace as I journey toward real healing and transformation, *As It Pleases You.*

    Father, I confess the moments when I have felt discomfort at another's success, or when I have struggled to celebrate the blessings of others while yearning for my own. I admit that, at times, I have resented what others possess, whether it is relationships, achievements, qualities, or opportunities. I ask You to forgive me for allowing envy and jealousy to take root in my heart, for these emotions have clouded my perspective, stifled my gratitude, and hindered my ability to love as You command.

    Holy Spirit, I invite You to search the depths and corners of my psyche. Reveal the hidden seeds and roots of envy and jealousy, whether they come from past hurts, insecurities, or misguided beliefs about scarcity. Shine Your light on any area where I compare myself to others, or where I measure my worth by the standards of the world instead of the truth of Your Word. Help me to understand the origin of these feelings so I can uproot them and break every yoke that binds me or cut every cord that has me entangled.

    Lord, Your Word teaches that where envy and self-seeking exist, there is confusion and every evil thing, but the Divine Wisdom that comes from above is pure, peaceable, and full of mercy. Grant me the courage to face the uncomfortable truths about myself without hiding or rationalizing them.

Free me from dishonesty and denial, and help me to pinpoint the real emotions and needs beneath my envy or jealousy.

Father, I pray for the Spirit of Compassion toward myself and others. When I am tempted to compare, remind me that my journey is unique and Divinely Designed with a personalized Spiritual Blueprint that is unmatched by another. Teach me to celebrate the victories of others without feeling threatened or diminished. Fill me with gratitude for the blessings I have received, and open my eyes to see the abundance in my own life.

Help me to resist the urge to measure my worth by my possessions, relationships, or outward success. Instead, anchor my identity in Your Divine Love and in the Spiritual Gifts You have placed within me. Guide me in discovering my own Blueprinted Purpose and fulfilling it with faithfulness. At the same time, knowing that Your Divine Timing is perfect and Your Predestined Plans are for my good and the Greater Good of all mankind.

Holy Spirit, when I am waiting for my own breakthrough, help me to trust You and to remain steadfast in hope. Guard my heart from all bitterness, hatefulness, and resentment. Release me from the grip of my negative emotions that erode my peace, health, and relationships. Renew my mind so that I may see others as fellow brethren on this journey, each with their own struggles, training, instructions, and blessings.

Father, I ask for the strength to take intentional steps toward Spiritual Growth, while Spiritually Tilling (Cultivating) my own ground. Allow me to ask myself honest questions, to seek the root causes of my feelings, and to embrace self-awareness as a path to freedom. Show me how to communicate with love, to be patient with myself, and to focus on personal growth rather than comparison. Transform my envy and jealousy into compassion, admiration, and inspiration.

Thank You for the promise that, as I surrender these emotions to You, You will reset my Mind, Body, Soul, and Spirit. I trust in Your ability to untangle every web of confusion and to fill my life with peace and contentment. May I become a Divine Vessel and Spiritual Conduit of Your Heavenly Love and Grace. My Lord, help me to celebrate the joys of others while waiting with hope for my own. In Jesus' Name I pray, Amen.

PRAYER OVERRIDE 31

The Mark of Favoritism

Heavenly Father, I come before You with a sincere heart, seeking Your Everlasting Wisdom and Divine Guidance as I reflect upon *The Mark of Favoritism*. Lord, I acknowledge that favoritism is a subtle yet powerful force that can shape families, relationships, communities, and even nations. I recognize its double-edged nature and the pain it causes when wielded with unrighteous motives. I ask You to search my heart and reveal any hidden areas where I have shown partiality, whether knowingly or unknowingly, so I may repent and be made right with You.

Father, Your Word reminds me that showing partiality is a sin, and I do not want to grieve Your Spirit or turn away from Your standard of righteousness. Help me to operate in the Spirit of Righteousness and keep my hands clean, even when I am overlooked, insulted, or mistreated. Grant me the grace to respond with humility and Christlike Character Traits in every circumstance, regardless of how others treat me.

Lord, I thank You that Your favor is just, fair, and non-discriminatory. You reward obedience and allow me to experience the consequences of disobedience, but You always do so with perfect justice and love. I ask You to purify my heart so that I may pursue Your Divine Will above my own desires and operate out of a heart aligned with Yours.

Holy Spirit, help me to see every person I encounter as worthy of kindness, respect, and fairness. Teach me to extend compassion to those who may never offer anything in return. Remove any desire within me to use others for selfish gain or to elevate myself at the expense of another. Guard my heart from pride, ego, and manipulation. Fill me with a Spirit of Selflessness, so that favor may flow through me as a blessing to others, not as a tool for personal advantage.

Father, when I encounter partiality in the world, empower me to respond with wisdom, patience, and love. Let me not become bitter or resentful when

I am on the receiving end of unfairness, but let me walk humbly, trusting that my worth and my Divine Destiny are determined by You alone. When I am granted favor, let me steward it with gratitude and generosity, always seeking to serve rather than to be served.

God, I ask that You transform my mind so that I may think, speak, and act in ways that PLEASE You. Let my words be seasoned with grace, and my actions be rooted in love and justice. Help me to align my life with Your Divine Principles and to exhibit the Fruits of the Spirit in all that I do. Show me the opportunities to encourage, affirm, and uplift others, especially those who are often overlooked or marginalized.

Holy Spirit, I surrender my motives and desires to You. Create in me a clean heart and renew a right Spirit within me. Give me the willingness to serve with humility, obedience, and joy, knowing that true favor comes from walking in ALIGNMENT with Your Divine Will, *As It Pleases You.* Guide me to foster environments of peace, inclusion, and kindness, reflecting the Kingdom of God in every sphere of my influence.

Thank You, Lord, for the continual process of transformation that You bring about in my life. As I surrender my thoughts, words, actions, and reactions to You, may Your Spirit REWIRE my heart and mind, empowering me to honor You and BLESS others, for I am indeed BLESSED to be a BLESSING. Let my life be a TESTIMONY of Your Divine Justice, Mercy, and Love. In Jesus' Name I pray, Amen.

PRAYER OVERRIDE 32

The Mark of Fear

Heavenly Father, I come before You acknowledging the presence and power of fear in my life. I confess that at times, I have allowed fear to break my focus, cloud my sense of good judgment, and distract me from walking confidently in the Predestined Purpose that You have set before me. I recognize that fear, though sometimes useful for protection, can become a chain that binds my Mind, Body, Soul, and Spirit, preventing me from moving forward in faith and fulfilling my Divine Calling, *As It Pleases You.*

Lord, Your Word reminds me that I am Spiritually Sealed with the Holy Spirit of Promise. It also reminds me that my true identity and protection come from the Divine Seal of the Heavenly of Heavens; therefore, I do not want to live out of alignment or in rebellion to You. Instead, I desire to be Spiritually Sealed, walking in obedience, truth, and righteousness, *As It Pleases You.* I ask You to search my heart and reveal any place where fear has taken hold, whether it is the fear of the unknown, the fear of failure, the fear of rejection, or any fear that keeps me from trusting fully in You.

Father, I surrender every hidden and spoken fear to You. I repent for entertaining thoughts that magnify my worries or diminish my confidence in Your Eternal Promises. I ask for forgiveness for any negative words or word curses I have spoken over my life or allowed others to speak over me. Help me to guard my mind and heart from the voices of doom, gloom, and discouragement. Replace every anxious thought with Your truth and peace.

Holy Spirit, empower me to choose faith over fear, obedience over convenience, and truth over deception. Remind me daily that I am not marked by fear, but by Your love, power, and sound mind. When I feel weak or overwhelmed, help me to seek comfort in Your presence, to cast my cares upon You, and to rest in the assurance that I am never alone.

Lord, I pray for the strength to discipline my mind and body, to remain focused and grateful, and to resist the temptation to settle for less than Your best. Teach me to recognize the origins of my fears, to forgive where there is hurt, and to surrender control of what I cannot change. Guide me to shift my focus from what I fear to what I can do, trusting You with every outcome.

Father, I ask that You break every cycle of unhealthy coping mechanisms that fear may produce in my life. Free me from the patterns of avoidance, negativity, and self-doubt. Cover me with the Blood of Jesus, and let Your Spirit lead me into wholeness and confidence. Show me practical ways to counteract fear, whether through prayer, Biblical Scriptures, positive actions, or acts of faith.

Holy Spirit, help me to own my fears, understand their roots or seeds, and release them into Your hands. Fill me with courage, laughter, hope, and the assurance that nothing can separate me from Your Heavenly and Organic Love. May I learn to REVERSE ENGINEER my fears, maximizing my BIRTHRIGHT of Spiritual Duality and Divine Dominion. While, at the same time, using all of my fears as stepping stones to erect the Divine Cornerstone of Faith, Wisdom, Understanding, Kindness, and Compassion, *As It Pleases You* on a Supernatural Level.

Thank You, Lord, for the Divine Seal of Protection, Identity, and Belonging that You have placed upon my life for my Heaven on Earth Experiences. In Earthen Vessel, I trust that as I lean into You, *Spirit to Spirit*, fear will lose its grip, and confidence will take its rightful place within my Mind, Body, Soul, and Spirit. May I live each day with boldness and joy, free from the marks of fear and frailty, and ready to fulfill my purpose for the Greater Good. In Jesus' Name I pray, Amen.

PRAYER OVERRIDE 33

The Mark of Frailty

Heavenly Father, I come before You with a humble heart, acknowledging my frailties and recognizing the moments where my weaknesses have threatened to define my path. I confess that the cracks in my confidence have sometimes caused me to make choices out of fear, regret, impulsion, lack, or confusion, allowing the adversary to sow seeds of doubt and disobedience in my Spirit. Yet, through Your Divine Grace and Mercy, I believe that every moment of vulnerability holds the hidden potential for strength, wisdom, and transformation.

Lord, I thank You for the examples You have given in Your Word, letting me know that no one is exempt from moments of frailty. What I gleaned is that those who stumbled, faltered, or struggled with their own marks of frailty rose above them by Your Spirit while operating in obedience and *As It Pleased You*. I see myself in their stories, knowing that my stumbles do not disqualify me from Your Everlasting Love or Your Predestined Purpose.

As I gather the pieces of my life, moving in Purpose on purpose, help me to see the areas I once considered as liabilities and reverse engineer them into assets. For I know that the very places You intend to reveal Your Divine Assets, Power, and Glory will be hidden in my perceived liabilities; therefore, as I become a work-in-progress, I am extracting and converting all of my frailties into Divine Lessons to feed Your precious sheep, *As It Pleases You*.

Holy Spirit, teach me to guard my words, emotions, and thoughts to prevent *The Mark of Frailty* from placing me in a known or unknown chokehold. As I cover myself with the Blood of Jesus, I am reminded that there is POWER in the words I release into the atmosphere, thus I govern them accordingly, *As It Pleases You*. Let me not be swayed by the negativity that surrounds me, but instead fill my mind and speech with encouragement, truth, and faith. Where I have spoken defeat or entertained thoughts of failure, I repent. I also ask for forgiveness as You help me to REWIRE my mindset toward hopefulness, the possibilities of greatness, and the unwavering resilience to move forward in the Spirit of Excellence.

Father, I surrender every area of weakness, every painful memory, every known or unknown trauma, and every regret to You. Show me how to fill the cracks in my confidence with Your Enduring Love and the PROMISES of Your Word. Give me the courage to peel back the layers of my own fragility and to discover the strength that lies beneath them. Help me to remember that my mistakes do not define me, but the redemptive work of Christ Jesus helps me to seek out my own SALVATION.

Lord, I ask for the discipline to renew my mind and heart daily. Guide me as I identify my old patterns of thoughts and behaviors that no longer serve You, as You grant me the willingness to embrace positive and effective change. Open my heart to revelatory knowledge and wisdom, so I may learn from every lesson and move forward with understanding, compassion, and humility.

Holy Spirit, grant me the perseverance to keep moving even when I feel inadequate or overwhelmed. I am reminded that consistency is more powerful than brilliance and that faithfulness in the small things leads to GREATNESS in Your Kingdom. Help me to document my Spiritual Journey, to ensure I do not forget things, to celebrate my progress, and to extend grace to myself and others as I grow.

Father, I thank You for the Divine Gift of Neuroplasticity, the ability to rewire or reorganize my brain and reshape my habits through Your Spirit. I embrace this process, however challenging it is, knowing that You are with me every step of the way. Let my life be a TESTAMENT to Your redemptive power, turning my weaknesses into strengths and my failures into victories.

Lord, I am committed to thinking, speaking, and behaving in ways that honor You and reflect the Fruits of the Spirit, *As It Pleases You*. I choose confidence over doubt, positivity over negativity, diligence over complacency, and faith over fear. As I move forward in the Spirit of Excellence, help me to break free from the unproductive and unfruitful boundaries and walls of my past and to step boldly into the future You have Divinely Prepared for me.

Thank You for never giving up on me and for loving me through every season of growth. May my frailties become the foundation upon which You build Divine Greatness. I trust You to lead me, transform me, and use every part of my story for Your Divine Glory. In Jesus' Name I pray, Amen.

PRAYER OVERRIDE 34

The Mark of Fixing People

Heavenly Father, I come before You with a heart seeking humility and wisdom as I reflect on *The Mark of Fixing People*. I confess that there have been times when I have assumed I knew what was best for others, speaking or acting from my own perceptions rather than Your Divine Word of Truth and Righteousness. Forgive me, Lord, for any confusion, unrest, or division I may have caused in the Body of Christ by trying to fix, judge, or control others without seeking the guidance of Your Spirit or the facts of their circumstances.

Holy Spirit, I surrender my need to fix others into Your hands. Teach me to listen with compassion, to ask questions with genuine curiosity, and to honor the journey that You have mapped out for every person. Help me to remember that only You truly know the depths of each heart and the plans You have for their lives. Where I have spoken out of turn or presumed to know Your Divine Will for someone else, I ask for forgiveness and restoration.

Lord, I pray for Divine Discernment and the ability to recognize the difference between Spirit-Led Guidance and self-driven intervention. Fill me with a Spirit of Love, Unity, and Patience, so that I may encourage and uplift my brothers and sisters rather than judge or control them. Remind me that declaring truth, as You lead, is different from imposing my own solutions or forcing change.

Father, protect me from falling into the trap of hypocrisy, self-righteousness, or violating the free will of another who is not my child. Help me to focus on cultivating my own heart, removing any planks from my eyes before offering help to others. Grant me the humility to receive correction, the grace to forgive, and the wisdom to offer support only when led by You.

Lord, I acknowledge that Your strategy is Divine, that You are the One who leads, restores, and delivers. Help me to trust in Your Divine Timing and Your process, whether it takes one day, forty days, or a lifetime. Teach me to honor the power of fasting, prayer, repentance, forgiveness, and obedience as You reveal them to me, as I allow Your Spirit to do the transforming work in all that I do, say, become, or engage in, *As It Pleases You*.

Holy Spirit, open my eyes to see as You see, to love as You love, and to serve as You serve. Guard me from pride, judgment, and the temptation to fix others for my own validation. Let my words and actions be filled with kindness, respect, and encouragement, always pointing others back to Your Kingdom.

Father, I thank You for the lessons of the past and the opportunity to learn from my mistakes. Give me a teachable Spirit, the willingness to grow, and the courage to admit when I am wrong. May I always choose love over criticism, unity over division, and Your Divine Will over my own.

Lord, as I interact with others in my Heaven on Earth Experiences, help me to be a Spiritual Vessel of healing, understanding, and compassion. Let me never lose sight of my own need for Your Divine Grace, as I freely share it with Your precious sheep. May my life reflect the beauty of Your Kingdom, and may I honor You in all I do, say, and think. In Jesus' Name I pray, Amen.

Dr. Y. Bur

www.DrYBur.com

PRAYER OVERRIDE 35

The Mark of Gossip

Heavenly Father, I come before You with a heart longing for purity in thought, speech, and action. I humbly confess that I have not always guarded my words with care, and at times I have allowed *The Mark of Gossip* to slip into my conversations. Lord, I admit that even when gossip begins as an innocent exchange or a subtle remark, it can quickly spiral into slander, judgment, and betrayal. I recognize that gossip wounds deeply, creating distrust, destroying relationships, and dividing families and communities.

Holy Spirit, I ask for Your conviction and guidance whenever I am tempted to speak or listen to words that do not honor others or bring glory to Your name. Make me sensitive to the nudges and red flags You place in my conscience, so I may pause and reconsider my words before they are spoken. Help me to set healthy boundaries in my conversations, choosing to honor the privacy and dignity of others.

Father, teach me to discern the motives behind my words properly. If I am tempted to spread information for curiosity, entertainment, or self-validation, remind me of the POWER of my tongue, which is to build up or tear down. Help me to remember that true concern is shown in prayer, support, and encouragement, not in spreading rumors or exposing another's struggles to make me feel better or more superior.

Lord, give me the wisdom and courage to change the subject, to walk away, or to gently redirect conversations that do not honor You or the people involved. Show me how to use my voice to bring healing, unity, and life instead of discord and suspicion. Let my words reflect compassion, respect, and maturity, marking me as one who brings peace wherever I go.

Holy Spirit, transform my heart so that I may delight in speaking good, positive, and uplifting things about others. Fill me with compassion for those who have been hurt by gossip, and grant me the humility to seek forgiveness if I have caused pain. Help me to be a safe place for others, honoring their stories and guarding their trust.

Father, I thank You for the lessons learned from both my mistakes and my efforts to do better. Help me to learn and grow, to stand on guard against negative projections, and to become an Authentic Vessel of Divine Wisdom and Understanding. Let me stand firm in my commitment to bring forth only what is true, noble, and beneficial, *As It Pleases You*.

Lord, may my words sow seeds of healing, restoration, and hope, counteracting *The Mark of Gossip* with real lovingkindness. Guide me each day to speak with intention and to live in such a way that my character reflects the Heart of Christ. In Jesus' Name I pray, Amen.

PRAYER OVERRIDE 36

The Mark of Greed

Almighty Father, I come before You acknowledging Your Holiness and Sovereignty over all creation. I thank You for the privilege to approach Your Heavenly Throne and bring before You the burdens and struggles that weigh on my heart. Today, I confess that *The Mark of Greed* is not a distant concept, but a subtle snare that can entangle my soul, often without my conscious awareness.

Lord, I admit that greed often disguises itself in my life, masquerading as ambition, prudence, or even self-care. I recognize that the Spirit of Selfishness seeks to take root in my heart, leading me to justify my actions that do not honor You or reflect Your Word. I confess my tendency to place my own desires, comfort, and recognition above Your Divine Will and above the needs of others. My Heavenly Father, I repent and ask that You forgive me for every moment I have denied the promptings of Your Spirit and chosen my own way.

I humbly ask You to shine the light of Your truth into the hidden corners of my heart. Reveal every attitude, thought, or desire that is driven by greed or selfishness. Help me to see myself clearly, not through the lens of self-justification, but through the Profound Wisdom of Your Word. Let me not be deceived by the world's standards or by my own rationalizations, but instead, let me be transformed by the renewing of my mind in Christ Jesus.

Father, I ask that You uproot every manifestation of greed from my life. Where I have prioritized my desires over Your Divine Purpose for my life, I surrender afresh to my Predestined Blueprint. Where I have withheld compassion, resources, or forgiveness, I ask for Your grace to help me extend generosity, kindness, and mercy. Where I have sought after praise, status, or recognition, redirect my focus to seek only Your approval. May I never withhold what You have called me to give. May I never judge others harshly, but instead, walk in humility and empathy, remembering the grace I have received.

Lord, I realize that greed is not simply a matter of money or possessions, but a Spirit that seeks to dominate my thoughts, decisions, and actions. I renounce the Spirit of Greed and the Spirit of Selfishness. I ask, Holy Spirit, that You fill every empty space within me with Your Holy Presence. Replace my self-centeredness with a Spirit of Generosity, my pride with a Spirit of Humility, and my insatiable desire for more with a Spirit of Contentment. My Lord, teach me how to be satisfied and to find my fulfillment in a *Spirit to Spirit* relationship with You, my Heavenly Father.

In Earthen Vessel, I pray for wisdom to recognize the ways in which greed tries to operate in my life. Empower me to question my motives, examine my heart and mind, and pursue a posture that reflects Your character. Grant me the courage to admit my faults, to seek reconciliation where I have caused harm, and to walk in obedience to Your Spiritual Principles and Standards. Let my life bear witness to Your transforming power, so that others do not see *The Mark of Greed*, but *The Mark of Christ* in me.

I thank You, Lord, that You are sufficient as Your mercy is renewed every morning. As You guard my heart from the invisible yoke of greed and selfishness, lead me into the freedom of Your Everlasting Love. Help me to love others as You have loved me, to be generous as You are generous, and to live each day with open hands and a surrendered heart. In Jesus' Name I pray, Amen.

PRAYER OVERRIDE 37

The Mark of Grouping (Stereotyping)

Heavenly Father, I come before You with a humble heart, recognizing Your Divine Sovereignty and Supernatural Wisdom above all things. I acknowledge that You alone can truly see into the depths of every heart, and You understand the unique journey of each of Your children. I confess that, as a Spiritual Being having a human experience, I have often fallen into the trap of grouping others, making judgments, and forming stereotypes that are not PLEASING in Your sight.

Lord, I admit that I have sometimes categorized people and situations in ways that serve my own comfort or understanding, rather than seeking Your truth and Your Divine Perspective. I repent for every time I have allowed the Spirit of Grouping and the Spirit of Stereotyping to take root within me, creating division, judgment, or indifference toward others. Forgive me for every moment I have failed to see others as You see them, beloved and precious in Your Divine Eye.

Father, I ask that You break every chain of mental or emotional slavery within me. I recognize that true freedom is not found in worldly status or outward appearances, but in the renewing of my mind and the alignment of my Spirit with Your Divine Will. Deliver me from the bondage of pretense, comparison, and the exhausting pursuit of approval. Help me to surrender my thoughts, ambitions, and self-imposed limitations to Your transforming power.

Lord, I surrender my tendency to judge, categorize, and stereotype. I ask for the courage to own my shortcomings and the grace to walk in humility. Help me to cultivate empathy, compassion, and understanding for those who are different from me, knowing that we are all Your children, created in Your Divine Image and deeply loved by You.

Holy Spirit, I invite You to search my heart and expose every area where I have allowed *The Mark of Grouping* to shape my thoughts, attitudes, or actions. Transform my mind so that I may see others through Your Divine Lens. Empower me to break free from every form of Spiritual and mental bondage that keeps me from walking in the fullness of my Divine Purpose. Where I have allowed distractions to pull me away from You, bring me back to the center of Your Divine Will.

Father, teach me to embrace my unique identity in Christ, while honoring the uniqueness of others. I fully understand that my true freedom begins in the mind, as I yield my thoughts and desires to the Body of Christ, *As It Pleases You*. Help me to release every pretense and to walk in genuine authenticity, trusting that Your Spirit will guide me into all truth.

Lord, I thank You for the process of change, growth, and renewal that You have embedded in my Spiritual DNA. I ask for the willingness and obedience to participate fully, as You lead me into greater maturity and alignment with You, *Spirit to Spirit*. Where I have been part of the problem, give me the courage to become part of the solution. Where I have wandered in Spiritual Deserts, grant me the faith and boldness to confront my inner giants and to possess the PROMISES, *As It Pleases You*.

Father, I pray for the strength to reject the lies of division, oppression, and self-deception. Fill me with a Spirit of Unity, Peace, and Love for all of mankind. Help me to use my words and actions to build up, not to tear down. May my life reflect the character of Christ, and may I always seek to PLEASE You in all things.

In Earthen Vessel for my Heaven on Earth Experiences, I surrender my mind, my will, and my heart to You. Mold me into a Spiritual Vessel of Your Divine Grace and Truth. Let me be a witness to the transforming power of Your Spirit, so that others may see You inside of me and be drawn to Your Divine Light. In Jesus' Name I pray, Amen.

PRAYER OVERRIDE 38

The Mark of Hatefulness

Gracious Father, I bow before You, coming out of the shadows with a heart open to Your Divine Illumination. I confess that, though I desire to be the loving one, there have been moments when *The Mark of Hatefulness* has negatively pierced my thoughts, words, or actions. I admit that, at times, I have harbored resentment, unforgiveness, or bitterness, sometimes even cloaked in civility or pretense. I recognize that I can only choose to be loving or hateful, and today, I choose love, even as I acknowledge that I am still a work-in-progress.

Lord, I ask that You expose every hidden root or seed of hatefulness within me. Shine Your Divine Light on any unresolved anger, bitterness, or offense that lingers in my heart. Search me, O God, and know my heart; try me, and know my anxieties. Reveal to me any attitudes, desires, or actions that have aligned with the Spirit of Hatefulness, so that I may confess them and turn away from them.

Holy Spirit, I invite You to cleanse my heart and mind. I repent for every time I have allowed hatred, animosity, or a desire for revenge to take hold of me. I repent for every word spoken in anger, every gesture made with ill intent, and every thought that has fueled division or pain. I renounce the Spirit of Hatefulness and every negative companion that travels with it, declaring that it no longer has a place in my repertoire.

Father, I forgive myself and anyone who has hurt me. I release all bitterness, wrath, anger, clamor, evil speaking, and malice, as Your Word commands. I choose to be kind, tenderhearted, and forgiving, just as You in Christ have forgiven me. I ask that Your Spirit would heal every wound and restore every place in me that has been damaged by hatefulness, whether given or received.

Lord, I proclaim my freedom and healing in Christ Jesus. I affirm that I am a new creation, empowered to love as You love. Let Your Spirit of Unity fill me, guiding me to exhibit the Fruits of the Spirit and to reflect Christlike Character Traits in all that I do. May my life be a TESTIMONY to the transforming power of Your love, astounding all who encounter me.

Help me to speak and walk in Your Predestined Promises, leaving no stone unturned. From this point forward, I am no longer a captive to hatefulness or any other negative characteristic. When I am wronged, give me grace to forgive and the courage to address the Spirit behind the offense. As I release all negativity, may Your Divine Peace guard my Mind, Body, Soul, and Spirit.

Father, I pray for healing in my life, my home, my community, and my nation. Let Your Spirit of Love overcome every trace of hatefulness, and let unity, mercy, and compassion flow freely among us. Use me as an instrument of peace and restoration, committed to protecting the innocent, restoring the lost, and addressing every issue at its root.

Thank You, Lord, for searching my heart and leading me in the everlasting way. Let my words and actions reflect the transformation that Your Spirit is working on within me to ultimately PLEASE You. In Jesus' Name I pray, Amen.

Dr. Y. Bur

www.DrYBur.com

PRAYER OVERRIDE 39

The Mark of Hiding

Heavenly Father, I come before You with sincerity and humility, recognizing that *The Mark of Hiding* has often shaped the way I interact with myself, with others, and with You. I acknowledge my tendency to hide when I am wounded, afraid, or uncertain. Sometimes, I hide deep within myself, concealing my true thoughts, feelings, and memories, even from my own conscious awareness. Other times, I mask my true identity from the world, presenting a version of myself that is not authentic, all in an effort to avoid judgment, rejection, trauma, or pain.

Lord, I realize that these patterns of hiding, both internal and external, can become barriers to my personal and Spiritual Growth, *As It Pleases You*. I confess that I have allowed my psyche to shield me from uncomfortable truths, hindering the healing and transformation You desire for me. I admit that I have sometimes used people, places, or things to cover my insecurities, rather than seeking refuge in You, *Spirit to Spirit*.

Father, I ask that You shine Your Divine Light into the hidden places of my heart. Reveal to me anything within me that is holding me back from walking in the fullness of my Predestined Blueprinted Purpose. Where I have hidden behind fear, hurt, or shame, I usher in Your Supernatural Healing Process. Where I have masked my true self to fit in or to avoid pain, give me the courage to embrace my authentic self.

Holy Spirit, I invite You into my life to cleanse my heart and mind. Purge me of every negative thought, habit, desire, or behavior that keeps me separated from God, my Heavenly Father. Help me to recognize when I am withdrawing for the wrong reasons and empower me to step out in faith, seeking Your face above all else. My Lord, grant me the Spiritual Discernment needed to know when to seek solitude for Spiritual Renewal and when to resist isolation that leads to Spiritual Dryness or Deprivation.

Lord, I acknowledge that my adversary prowls like a roaring lion, seeking to devour those who are vulnerable or isolated. For this reason, keep me sober and vigilant, rooted in Your Divine Truth, while being quick to RECOGNIZE, REJECT, or CANCEL any agreement containing negative character traits, debauched fruits, or ungodly projections that are not of You. In Earthen Vessel, as I walk in Willful Agreement with You, my Heavenly Father, according to Your Word, Spiritual Principles, and Divine Standards, close every door that I have inadvertently opened to the adversary to yoke, sift, or distract me.

Father, I receive Your invitation to Spiritual Cleansing. Just as I bathe my physical body to remove unseen dirt, so I ask for Your living water to cleanse my Spirit. Wash away every residue of negativity, fear, and shame that has attached itself to me. Purify my motives, my thoughts, and my environment. I choose to protect the positive energy You have placed within me and to resist the influence or the penetration of negativity.

In Earthen Vessel, I commit to repentance, forgiveness, fasting, worship, and prayer as my means of Spiritual Cleansing. In addition, my Lord, *Spirit to Spirit*, I ask for the Supernatural Strength to cast out every negative Spirit and habit that hinders my growth or prevents me from feeding Your precious sheep, *As It Pleases You*. In doing so, for my Heaven on Earth Experience, while being in Purpose on purpose, I am reminded that I am never alone. For Your Spirit is within me, doing what it is designed to do, as I cover myself with the Blood of Jesus as my Spiritual Atonement, anointing the DOORPOST of my Mind, Body, Soul, and Spirit.

Lord, let me walk in the Spirit of Righteousness, not allowing *The Mark of Hiding* to limit my calling or my ability to serve You. Replace my hiding with HOLY BOLDNESS and my fear with faith. Help me to be transparent with myself, with others, and most of all, with You. Let my life be a reflection of Your Divine Light, free from the shadows of secrecy or shame.

Thank You, my Heavenly Father, for Your unending mercy and for the transformative power of Your Spirit. I trust that as I seek You, I will find healing, restoration, and the courage to live openly and honestly before You and the world. In Jesus' Name I pray, Amen.

PRAYER OVERRIDE 40

The Mark of Idolatry

Almighty God, I come before You in awe and reverence, seeking understanding and freedom from *The Mark of Idolatry*. I acknowledge that You alone are worthy of my worship, devotion, and honor. I confess that, knowingly and unknowingly, I have placed other things, people, desires, and even my own ambitions above You. I recognize that idolatry is not always a golden statue or a tangible object, but can be anything that takes Your rightful place in my heart and mind.

Father, I ask You to search the depths of my soul and reveal to me any secret idols that I have allowed to form within my psyche. Shine Your Divine Light, exposing every area where I have misplaced my devotion, where I have sought fulfillment, confidence, or comfort outside of You. Show me the subtle ways that my pretense, hypocrisy, and the pursuit of status or fame have become substitutes for my authentic or unwavering faith and trust in You. Expose the golden calves that I have built, even if they are hidden in my habits, relationships, self-seeking approvals, or hidden insecurities.

Lord, I realize that my psyche, my mind, will, emotions, and intellect are designed to serve You, not the self-created altars for my pleasure or to the things of this world. I repent for every time I have pretended to possess Divine Power or have constructed false narratives to hide my doubts and weaknesses. I surrender my longing for control, comfort, and tangible assurance, and I ask You to fill the void within me with Your Divine Presence and Your Holy Truth.

Holy Spirit, I invite You to cleanse my heart, renew my mind, and refocus my desires. Help me to stand in authentic faith, trusting in Your unseen yet unshakable power. Guard me from the known and unknown temptation to idolize people, my possessions, my achievements, or even my own image. Strengthen my steadfastness in worshipping You and You alone, to seek You above all else, and to allow no substitute to take root in my life.

Father, teach me to recognize when I am drifting from my Predestined Purpose or conforming to worldly patterns. When I face the temptation to idolize anything or anyone, remind me of the example of David, who remained steadfast in Your Divine Purpose with a repentant heart and Supernatural Protection. Help me to lay aside every idol, whether obvious or disguised, and to put on the Whole Armor of God so that I may stand firm in the face of every challenge, distraction, or attack.

Lord, I ask that You pin every spear meant for my destruction to the wall, just as You did for Your servants in times past. I declare that Your Divine Power and Everlasting Righteousness will consume every evil rod contending against Your Divine Will or my Predestined Blueprinted. Deliver me from the grip of trauma, fear, and conformity, and renew my mind as I offer myself wholly to You.

Thank You for Your Unwavering Mercy and for the Gift of Transformation. Fill every longing, thirst, and void within me with Your Uncommon Love, Your Holy Truth, Your Holy Spirit, and the Blood of Jesus. Let my life be a LIVING TESTIMONY of my devotion to You as I am freed in my Mind, Body, Soul, and Spirit from the chains of idolatry. In Jesus' Name I pray, Amen.

Dr. Y. Bur

www.DrYBur.com

PRAYER OVERRIDE 41

The Mark of Impatience

Heavenly Father, I come before You with a heart that longs for peace and transformation. I acknowledge that impatience has often taken root in my life, shaping my thoughts, actions, words, and relationships in ways that do not honor You. I confess that many times I rush ahead, frustrated by delays and inconveniences, failing to pause and seek Your Divine Wisdom in the waiting process. I have allowed the Spirit of Impatience to influence my words and my decisions, sometimes hurting those I love and missing the deeper work, cleansing, and training You wish to do within me.

Lord, I recognize that impatience is not simply a fleeting feeling, but a revealing mirror of my mindset, my values, and my Spiritual Health. I see now that impatience can open the door to chaos, division, and woundedness, both in myself and in others. I repent for every moment I have allowed the Spirit of Impatience, the Spirit of Leviathan, or any other negative force to take precedence over the Fruit of Patience that Your Spirit desires to produce within me.

Father, I ask You to search my heart and reveal the seeds and roots of impatience. Expose the pride, entitlement, or unresolved trauma that keeps me negatively aggressive, striving, and reacting out of frustration. Cleanse me from every impulse that rushes past or against Your Divine Timing and Your Predestined Plans. Teach me to rest in You, to wait patiently for Your guidance, and to trust that Your ways are higher than mine.

Holy Spirit, I invite You to renew my mind and transform my heart. Empower me to recognize the signs of impatience as signals to draw closer to You, rather than acting out of frustration or annoyance. When I am tempted to speak harshly, to judge unfairly, or to make hasty decisions, remind me to pause, breathe, and seek Your Divine Wisdom first. Fill me with the Spirit of Patience, so that I may reflect Your character in every circumstance.

Lord, as of this moment, I surrender my desire for control, my need for instant results, my desire for instant gratification, and my tendency to compare my journey with others. Help me to find contentment in Your presence and to value the lessons found in waiting. Strengthen my relationships by teaching me to give time, attention, and compassion to those You have placed in my life. Where I have wounded others through impatience, grant me the humility to seek forgiveness and the grace to make amends.

Father, I declare that I will no longer allow impatience to shape my life. I cover every area of my heart and mind with the Blood of Jesus. I ask You to align my Mind, Body, Soul, and Spirit with Your Word and Your Divine Will. Let the Holy Spirit guide me, instruct me, and remind me of the power I hold in You to overcome every negative habit, thought, belief, word, action, or reaction.

Thank You for Your Everlasting Mercy and for the PROMISE of renewal. As I rise up from every dry place, let the Fruit of Patience blossom in my life, bringing peace, understanding, and strength to every Season, Cycle, and Vicissitude as I Spiritually Till (Cultivate) my own ground. Let my life be a TESTIMONY of Your transforming power, and may I always remember that true change begins from within and is sustained by Your Spirit. In Jesus' Name I pray, Amen.

PRAYER OVERRIDE 42

The Mark of Impulsion

Heavenly Father, I come before You with a heart yearning for Your Divine Wisdom and Spiritual Guidance. I acknowledge that *The Mark of Impulsion* has quietly shaped many areas of my life, sometimes in ways I do not even recognize. I confess that I have often acted on impulse, allowing my desires, fears, and habits to guide me instead of seeking Your counsel and waiting on Your Spiritual Nudge or Permission. I realize that my impulsions can influence my words, my thoughts, my desires, my actions, my relationships, and my decisions, sometimes drawing me away from Your Divine Purpose, *As It Pleases You.*

Lord, I ask You to search my heart and reveal every hidden impulse that does not align with Your Divine Will. Shine Your Illuminating Light on the emotional, physical, verbal, creative, social, financial, and Spiritual Impulses that seek to control me. Help me to recognize when my responses are born and bred out of habit, fear, or longing rather than faith, wisdom, and discernment. Teach me to surrender these impulses to You so that I may walk in the Spirit of Self-Control and Excellence.

Holy Spirit, I invite You to be my guide and my guard. Help me to pause, reflect, and seek Your Spiritual Direction before I speak, act, or decide. Strengthen me to resist the pull of impulsion and to cultivate the Fruit of Patience, understanding the power of waiting on You. Remind me that every giant or stronghold I face has a weakness, and that victory is found not by my own strength but by Your Divine Insight and Supernatural Power already residing within me.

Father, I repent for every moment I have given in to impulsion, opening doors to negative cycles in my life and in the lives of others. I ask for Your forgiveness and for the courage to break free from every generational curse, soul tie, or stronghold that keeps me from walking in the light of Your truth. I declare that I will not leave open doors for the enemy to exploit, but will prepare for freedom by filling my mind and heart with Your Word, prayer, fasting, worship, and repentance.

Lord, help me to use the Spiritual Gifts, Talents, and Tools You have given me with wisdom, humility, and skill. Teach me to build my character in the quiet places, just as David did, so that I may be prepared to face every challenge and lead with LOVE and INSIGHT, *As It Pleases You*. Remind me that, as Your sheep, I am called to LISTEN for Your Heavenly Voice above all others, to trust Your Divine Provisions, and to follow where You lead without fear or doubt.

My Way Maker, I choose to align my life with You, *Spirit to Spirit*. When impulsion calls me to rush, to react, or to take matters into my own hands, help me to pause, listen, and respond as You would have me respond. Let the Blood of the Lamb and the word of my TESTIMONY be my shield and my song, so that I may overcome every mark of impulsion and walk in lasting victory, *As It Pleases You*.

Thank You for being my Shepherd, my Savior, and my Sustainer. I trust that what belongs to me will come in Your perfect timing, and that I will never be forsaken as I follow You. Fill me with Supernatural Peace, Divine Discernment, and a Spirit of Self-control, so that my life may bear witness to Your transforming POWER and LOVE. In Jesus' Name I pray, Amen.

www.DrYBur.com

PRAYER OVERRIDE 43

The Mark of Individuality

Heavenly Father, Lord of all Creation, I come before You in awe of Your Divine Wisdom and Sovereignty. Thank You for lovingly crafting me according to Your Divine Blueprint, a work of art that bears Your signature. In a world that demands conformity and rewards imitation, I confess that I have at times struggled to embrace the *Divine Mark of Individuality* that You have placed upon my life, while taking on *The Mark of Individuality* from the adversary. I acknowledge that it is far too easy to seek validation from the crowd, to measure myself by earthly standards, and to forget that my true identity is found only in Christ Jesus.

Lord, deliver me from the whispers of insecurity and the temptations to compromise who You have called me to be. Remind me that I am fearfully and wonderfully made, called to stand out and not to blend in. When I am tempted to edit or erase the uniqueness You have written into my story, grant me the courage to trust in Your perfect design. Let me not labor to create my own blueprint, but to surrender wholeheartedly to the Divine Blueprint You have placed within me.

Just as You trained the patriarchs and prophets, teaching them the humility of shepherds, train my heart to listen to Your Heavenly Voice above all others. Free me from the whitewash mentality that seeks to erase the beauty of diversity among Your people. Help me understand that my battles are not for my own glory, nor for the shedding of innocent blood, but for the preservation of righteousness and the saving of souls.

Father, instill in me a readiness for Spiritual Battle, going toe to toe with the adversary. May I not wait until crisis comes to seek You, but instead walk daily in the Spiritual Armor of Faith, clothed in Your Authentic Truth and Abounding Love. Shape my character, as You shaped David's, to pursue Your heart above all else. Let my willingness to be righteous outweigh any imperfections, for You seek not outward perfection, but hearts willing to be transformed by Your Spirit.

I confess, Lord, that I have fallen short; I have wounded others in thought, word, and deed. I ask for the grace to recognize my failings, to repent sincerely, and to be made new by Your Divine Mercy. May I be honest about my shortcomings and eager to make the corrections needed to become a vessel fit for Your Divine Purpose and Supernatural Spiritual Power.

Root my identity in love, humility, honor, and gratitude. Teach me to value others not for what they can offer me, but simply because they are Your creation. Let my people skills reflect the holiness You desire, so that the contents of my heart bring glory to Your name when no one is watching.

Grant me Divine Wisdom, Lord, to treat even the least among us with dignity and respect. Keep me from empty rituals and from being swayed by material gain. Instead, let my heart be tender and teachable, always ready to follow the Good Shepherd, Jesus Christ, who laid down His life for His sheep.

When I am tempted to act without integrity, convict me by Your Spirit to examine the motives of my heart and the thoughts of my mind. Let my actions be led by truth and compassion, not self-interest or ambition. Remind me that I am known by You, chosen by You, and called to bring others into the FOLD of Your free will grace.

If disobedience finds a place in my life, reveal it to me swiftly so that I may REPENT and return to the path that PLEASES You. Thank You for the Spiritual Blueprint that guides me, a Spiritual Mark that cannot be erased by the world's uncertainty or my own doubts. I yield my will to Yours, trusting that Your Predestined Plan is perfect and Your love is unfailing. In Jesus' Name I pray, Amen.

PRAYER OVERRIDE 44

The Mark of Insaneness

Gracious Father, I come before You in a Spirit of Humility, recognizing the depths of my need for Your Holy Presence, *Spirit to Spirit*. At times, I feel as though the pressures of life are mounting beyond my capacity to bear. Responsibilities, memories, and emotions sometimes swirl in my mind, causing confusion and a sense that I am losing my grip. Yet even in my weakness, I know You are the God who sees, the God who knows, and the God who restores.

Lord, I confess the moments when I have questioned my worth or doubted Your good intentions for my life. When my thoughts are scattered, my emotions run high, and I am tempted to believe that I am beyond repair, remind me that You make no mistakes. You have crafted me with purpose and intention, and You have not given me a Spirit of Fear, but of power, love, and a sound mind. Help me reject every lie that says I am not enough, that I am forgotten, or that I am beyond Your reach.

Father, I acknowledge the marks of trauma, insecurity, and emotional scars that I may carry. I know I am not alone in these struggles, for every person bears their own burdens and battles. Give me discernment to recognize my triggers and wisdom to seek Your healing. Let me not hide or deny my weaknesses, but instead, bring them into the light of Your truth, trusting that Your Divine Grace is sufficient for me.

Protect me from the Spirit of Deception, which seeks to trap me in cycles of shame, sabotage, or falsehood. I ask You to fill me with the Spirit of Righteousness and Excellence, that I may stand firm in my identity as Your beloved child. Strengthen me to resist the urge to give up when life becomes overwhelming. Instead, teach me to pause, to rest in Your Divine Presence, and to be renewed by Your Spirit.

Lord, help me see that I am a work in progress, shaped by Your loving hands. Even when I falter or feel as though I am losing my mind, remind me that Your power is perfected in my weakness. Fill my heart with the assurance that You have entrusted me with Spiritual Gifts, Divine Wisdom, and a Predetermined Purpose not only for my own life, but for the BLESSING of others and to FEED Your precious sheep.

May I never allow the Spirit of Unrighteousness or Deception to build a nest in my mind or soul. If it has found a place, I ask You to cast it out with Your Supernatural Power and Presence. Guard my heart and mind with Your peace that surpasses all understanding. Let me be quick to recognize when I am straying from Your truth, and eager to return to the path You have set for me.

Father, grant me the courage to share my LESSONS and TESTIMONY with others, using my story to nourish and encourage those around me. Let me operate in the Spirit with integrity, never boasting, but always giving You the glory for every increase and every breakthrough. Teach me to discern what to share, when to share, and how to share, so that Your Divine Wisdom may flow through me in an Earthen Vessel for Your Kingdom.

Remind me that You alone are the Source of all supernatural power and protection. No person, circumstance, or force can hinder Your Divine Operation in my life unless I allow it. Keep me humble, Lord, always aware that every good gift is from You and that I am called to serve with a willing heart.

If I am ever tempted to walk away from my Divine Calling or take on the burden of insanity, arrest and convict my Spirit and draw me near to You, *Spirit to Spirit*. Help me to remember that to whom much is given, much is required. Let me not forfeit the BLESSINGS or responsibilities You have entrusted to me. Instead, strengthen me to persevere, to walk the narrow path, and to use my Spiritual Gifts as You intended.

Lord, I thank You for calling me out of darkness into Your marvelous light. Let me honor this calling by living boldly and authentically, never hiding from my challenges, but facing them with the assurance that You are with me. May Your Spirit lead me in every thought, word, and action, so that I may fulfill my purpose and bring glory. In Jesus' Name I pray, Amen.

PRAYER OVERRIDE 45

The Mark of Insecurity

Heavenly Father, I come before You with an open heart, acknowledging the struggle within me that is often hidden from the eyes of others. I confess that insecurity has, at times, colored my thoughts, shaped my actions, and influenced my relationships. You see beyond my outward composure and into the depths of my soul, where the roots of my fears and doubts reside. I thank You that I do not have to hide or pretend in Your Divine Presence, for You are the One who knows me completely and loves me unconditionally.

Lord, I ask for the courage to face *The Mark of Insecurity* that seeks to undermine my confidence and erode my trust in You. I surrender every mask of perfectionism, defensiveness, judgment, and pretense that I have worn to hide my struggles. Help me to recognize that insecurity is not always shyness or self-doubt, but can take many forms, even those that appear strong or assertive. Teach me to discern when I am operating in the Spirit of Negativity, and give me the wisdom to turn away from my negative attitude, words, desires, or actions that harm myself or others.

Father, I invite Your Healing Spirit into my loins to search my heart and mind to reveal the places where insecurity has taken root. Where I have allowed it to create distance in my relationships, to make me rude, mean, or toxic, I ask for forgiveness and for the grace to make amends. Where my need for validation or control has hindered my intimacy or trust, help me to learn humility and surrender. I understand that my achievements and the opinions of others do not determine my worth; it is ultimately determined by Your Divine Love and the identity I have in Christ Jesus.

Lord, I confess that I have sometimes appeared confidently secure on the outside while wrestling with uncertainty within. I have sought affirmation from those around me, taken credit that was not mine, or used others to fill the voids in my heart. I ask for the strength to exchange the exhausting pursuit of approval for the peace of genuine self-acceptance. Let me become someone who builds others up, rather than tearing them down, who encourages and serves, rather than competes or belittles.

Father, help me to embrace my weaknesses as opportunities for Your strength to be revealed. Teach me to rest in Your sufficiency and to trust that You have made me fearfully and wonderfully, with a unique purpose and calling. Let my confidence be rooted in who You are and who I am in You, not in fleeting circumstances or the shifting opinions of others.

Shape me into a person who is confidently secure, whose assurance is founded on Your truth and faithfulness. May my life be marked by kindness, humility, and a willingness to serve, rather than by arrogance or criticism. Fill me with the Spirit of Encouragement, so I may lift others up and reflect the love of Christ in all that I do.

Lord, keep me from the trap of comparison and the poison of insecurity. Renew my mind with Your Word, and let the Spirit of Truth guard my heart against every lie that would diminish my value. Teach me to celebrate the successes of others and to walk in gratitude for the gifts You have given me. Thank You for the gift of self-acceptance and for the freedom that comes from knowing I am Yours. Help me to extend that same grace and acceptance to others, building a community marked by love, support, and authenticity.

I trust that You are transforming me from the inside out, freeing me from *The Mark of Insecurity* and establishing me in the confidence that comes from You alone. In Jesus' Name I pray, Amen.

PRAYER OVERRIDE 46

The Mark of Insulting Others

Heavenly Father, I come before You with a Spirit of Humility and Reflection. I recognize that my words hold power, and I confess that there have been times when I have spoken carelessly or allowed *The Mark of Insulting Others* to take root in my heart. I repent for every moment when I have used my words to wound, belittle, or cast judgment upon another, whether out of anger, jealousy, bitterness, or pride. You see the motives of my heart, and I ask for Your forgiveness for every negative word I have spoken, whether openly or in secret.

Lord, I ask You to cleanse my heart of any desire for defamatory fame or toxic validation. Help me see that exposing the flaws or failures of others to boost myself only contaminates my Spirit and distances me from Your Divine Favor. Let my reputation be built on love, honesty, and uplifting others, not on the pain or embarrassment of those around me. Remove the urge to mock, accuse, or insult You, myself, or others. Instead, fill me with the Spirit of Compassion, Love, and Understanding, *As It Pleases You.*

Father, I acknowledge that negative energy is real and that the atmosphere I create with my words and actions affects both myself and those around me. Teach me to be an agent of peace, choosing kindness over criticism and encouragement over condemnation. When I encounter difficult or negative situations, grant me the Divine Wisdom and Abounding Grace to shift the atmosphere with uplifting words, gentle humor, honest apologies, and sincere compliments. Let my presence bring light and comfort, not discomfort, discord, or division.

Lord, I ask You to help me respect the free will of every person I encounter. Remind me that it is not my place to control, manipulate, or override the choices of others. Give me the humility to lead by example, to offer guidance and support without force, and to release others into Your care when they refuse to listen or accept what I have to share. Let me never violate the boundaries You have set, but instead honor the gift of free will as You do, fostering authentic and healthy relationships.

Teach me to be clear in my words and intentions. When I find myself in a fog of confusion or uncertainty, help me to pause, seek clarity, and align my thoughts and actions with Your Spirit. Guide me to take ownership of my words, eliminate excuses, and understand the emotional attachments that influence my responses. Give me discernment to recognize when negativity threatens to cloud my mind, and grant me the strength to eliminate or limit its influence.

Father, in moments when I feel compelled to insult or tear down, stop me and fill my mouth with words of life and encouragement. Let me become a vessel of peace, healing, and restoration in every environment I enter. When I offend or hurt someone, give me the humility to apologize sincerely and to make amends, seeking always to build up rather than break down.

I pray that You would surround me with those who value clarity, kindness, and truth. Allow me to be a source of clarity and encouragement for others, just as You send people into my life to provide clarity for me. Help me to recognize when I need to step back, reflect, and free my mind from distractions or negativity. Guide me in developing habits and strategies that promote clarity, peace, and positive energy.

Lord, I thank You for the lessons life brings, even when they are uncomfortable or challenging. Use every experience to teach me, grow me, and draw me closer to You, *Spirit to Spirit*. May my life be marked not by *The Mark of Insulting Others*, but by the Mark of Kindness, Clarity, and Respect for the free will of every person I meet.

I trust that You are able to transform my heart and renew my mind, making me the Earthen Vessel fit and prepared for Your service to feed Your precious sheep. And, my Lord, make me a beacon of Divine Light in a world that desperately needs Your Abounding Love. In Jesus' Name I pray, Amen.

PRAYER OVERRIDE 47

The Mark of Interruptions

Heavenly Father, I come before You with a heart full of gratitude for the gift of my mind and the intricate ways You have designed me. I acknowledge that *The Mark of Interruptions* is woven into the fabric of my daily life. Sometimes I am the one who is interrupted, and other times I am the one who interrupts. I admit that these moments can lead to frustration, impatience, and even selfishness when I fail to honor the sacredness of my own mind and the minds of those around me.

Lord, I ask You to grant me discernment as I navigate the endless distractions and interruptions that seek to steal my focus and peace. Help me to recognize when an interruption is a Divine Appointment, a moment meant for connection, growth, or service. Teach me to welcome those interruptions that are sent by You, and to respond with grace, humility, and openness. At the same time, give me the strength and wisdom to set healthy boundaries, to guard my sacred time with You, and to protect moments of prayer, meditation, and reflection from unnecessary disturbances.

Father, I confess that there are times when I interrupt others, whether out of impatience, pride, or a desire to be heard. Forgive me for failing to listen with compassion and respect. Fill me with the Spirit of Patience and Understanding so that I may honor the voices and experiences of those around me. Transform my interactions so that I become a vessel of peace and encouragement, not a source of distraction or discord.

Lord, I recognize that many interruptions begin in my own mind. Wandering thoughts, worries, and memories can disrupt my focus and steal my clarity. I ask You to sanctify my thoughts, to help me take every thought captive, and to renew my mind by the power of Your Spirit. Let my mind be a sacred place where You can communicate with me, free from the clutter, negativity, and chaos of the world.

Father, remind me of the power and potential of the mind You have given me. Help me to release my self-imposed limitations and to be open to the new pathways and strengths You are waiting to reveal. Teach me to value my mind as a Divine Gift, not simply a tool for productivity or achievement, but as a vessel for Your Divine Wisdom, Creativity, and Presence, *As It Pleases You*.

In the moments of my mental fogs, confusion, or distractions, draw me back to a place of stillness, focus, and clarity. Show me how to pinpoint negativity and eliminate or limit its influence over my life. Guide me to set intentions that are aligned with Your Divine Will, to seek clarity in my thoughts, and to trust You with the outcomes beyond my control.

Lord, let me never forget that You are the ultimate source of Divine Wisdom and Authentic Power. Keep me alert and watchful, guarding my mind from the schemes of the enemy. May I use every interruption as an opportunity to grow in character, deepen my dependence on You, and reflect Your Everlasting Love and Authentic Patience to others.

Thank You for the sacredness of my mind and for the endless possibilities contained within it. I surrender my thoughts, interruptions, and distractions to You, asking that You use them to shape me and draw me ever closer to Your heart. Let my life be a living TESTIMONY of what it means to be transformed by the renewing of my Mind, Body, Soul, and Spirit. In Jesus' Name I pray, Amen.

PRAYER OVERRIDE 48

The Mark of Judgment

Heavenly Father, I come before You with a humble heart, seeking Your Divine Wisdom and Grace as I confront *The Mark of Judgment* in my own life. I acknowledge that I have been wounded by judgment, ridicule, and rejection, and I have also been guilty of judging others. The cycles, seasons, and challenges of life often tempt me to retaliate, harden my heart, or hide away from the lessons You intend for me to learn. Yet I know that every trial, every word spoken against me, and every moment of misunderstanding is an opportunity for Spiritual Growth and Refinement, *As It Pleases You.*

    Lord, I confess that at times I have failed to see the hidden lessons and treasures within the hurtful experiences I have endured. I have allowed the opinions of others to shape my self-worth, and I have sometimes closed the vault of my heart to both You and those around me. I ask for the courage to open that vault, to examine what I have locked inside of me. All of my fears, doubts, pains, traumas, and secrets, I bring them into the forefront for Divine Healing or Illumination, *As It Pleases You.* Teach me to own my truth with dignity and to understand the difference between wisdom and reckless disclosure. Help me to discern what must remain between You and me, *Spirit to Spirit*, and one to another with Your precious sheep.

    Father, I repent for the times I have judged others, whether openly or in secret. I confess that I have sometimes measured others by standards I myself could not meet, and spoken words that were not rooted in love, compassion, or truth. Forgive me for every moment of pride, prejudice, or hypocrisy. Fill me with the Spirit of Mercy and Understanding, so that I may see others as You see them and extend the same grace to them that I desire for myself.

    Lord, remind me that Your Divine Order governs the cycles and seasons of my life. Help me to sow good seeds, to act with integrity, and to trust that every harvest will be a reflection of Your Divine Justice and Love. When I am misunderstood, misjudged, or mistreated, grant me the strength to respond with patience and humility, knowing that You are my ultimate Judge and Defender.

Father, help me to examine the contents of my heart and to identify anything that blocks me from experiencing Your Divine Fullness. If fear, envy, bitterness, or unforgiveness lingers within me, I ask for the courage to confront and release it. If pride or deceit clouds my mind, purify me with Your Everlasting Truth. May I never hold onto anything that keeps me locked in Spiritual Stagnation, or what prevents me from moving forward in faith or in the Spirit of Excellence, *As It Pleases You.*

Teach me to live honestly, to speak with integrity, and to let my actions reflect the LOVE and RIGHTEOUSNESS of Christ. May I never use my testimony or my truth to wound others or to elevate myself at their expense. Show me how to share my experiences in a way that brings healing, hope, and encouragement, always seeking Your Divine Guidance before revealing what is meant to be kept between us.

Lord, let my life be marked not by judgment, but by the Fruit of the Spirit with Love, Joy, Peace, Patience, Kindness, Goodness, Faithfulness, Gentleness, and Self-Control. Help me to see every person, including myself, through Your Divine Eye. When I am tempted to judge, remind me of the grace and mercy I have received. When I face judgment from others, help me to respond with humility and trust in Your perfect justice.

Thank You for the lessons hidden in every trial, for the opportunity to grow stronger, wiser, and more compassionate, *As It Pleases You.* I surrender my heart, my vault, and my life to You, asking that You would unlock every area that needs Your Divine Healing and most Potent Touch. Use every experience to draw me closer to You, to shape my character, and to prepare me for the DESTINY You have designed for me. In Jesus' Name I pray, Amen.

PRAYER OVERRIDE 49

The Mark of Lies

Heavenly Father, I come before You seeking Your Divine Truth and Light in a world where deception, distortion, and falsehoods surround me on every side. I recognize that *The Mark of Lies* is not just something I encounter in others, but a struggle that resides within me as well. I confess that I have, at times, believed lies about myself, spoken untruths to others, or allowed the whispers of the enemy to cloud my mind and steal my peace.

Lord, I ask You to search my heart and mind posture, revealing every hidden place where falsehood has taken root or has seeded itself within my psyche. Expose the excuses, the procrastination, and the self-deceptions that keep me bound to cycles of delay, fear, and regret. Grant me the courage to face the lies I have told myself about my time, my purpose, and my worth. Help me to recognize when I am using busyness, distractions, or unhealthy habits as a cover-up or to avoid the truth You are calling me to embrace.

Father, I repent for every time I have allowed *The Mark of Lies* to dictate my actions, words, thoughts, or intentions. Forgive me for the times when I have chosen comfort over honesty, or when I have compromised my integrity for the sake of convenience, acceptance, or gain. Wash me clean from the Joker Spirit that seeks to manipulate, seduce, or deceive me, especially in my moments of weakness or need. Strengthen me to resist the urge to take shortcuts, to please others at the expense of my own values, or to present a false image to the world.

I ask for the discipline to honor my time as a Sacred Gift from You, my Heavenly Father. Teach me to manage my days with Divine Wisdom, Purpose, and Clarity, as I refuse to waste my precious moments with lies or excuses. Help me to respect the time of others as I respect my own, while cultivating the righteous habits of honesty, accountability, and stewardship. Where I have misused time or misrepresented my intentions, grant me the humility to acknowledge my mistakes and to make amends.

Lord, empower me to cast down every lie that undermines my calling, drains my joy, or clouds my vision. Fill me with the Spirit of Truth so that I may discern the difference between Your Divine Voice and the deceptive whispers of the enemy. Let Your Divine Wisdom guide my heart as You attune my mind with Your Divine Instructions and as You Spiritually Align my steps with Your Divine Purpose.

Father, I pray for Supernatural Protection against the Joker Spirit and every force that seeks to ensnare me in deception, manipulation, or self-betrayal. Guard my heart, my relationships, and my reputation with Your Divine Presence. Surround me with Wise Counsel and Divine Guidance, and keep me anchored in Your Word so that I will not be led astray.

Teach me to own my truth, to admit my mistakes, to apologize when I am wrong, and to learn the lessons You have placed before me. May I grow in stature and wisdom, embracing each experience as an opportunity to become more like Christ. Let me never settle for mediocrity or pretend to be someone I am not, but instead pursue authenticity, humility, and growth.

Lord, I surrender my time, my mind, and my intentions to You. Renew my Spirit with Your Divine Love, and empower me to rise above *The Mark of Lies*. Let my life be marked by honesty, truth, and a steadfast commitment to Your Divine Will. May I honor my Genius from Within and live each day with purpose, courage, and gratitude, knowing that You are guiding me every step of the way. In Jesus' Name I pray, Amen.

PRAYER OVERRIDE 50

The Mark of Low Self-Esteem

Heavenly Father, I come before You with an open heart, acknowledging the struggles I face with low self-esteem. Lord, You know my innermost thoughts, my silent doubts, and the ways I sometimes diminish my worth in the quiet of my soul. I admit that there are moments when self-doubt overwhelms me, causing me to question my abilities, my value, and even my place in the grand theme of things. I confess that at times I have allowed negative self-talk and a critical inner voice to shape my identity, rather than trusting in the truth of who You say I am.

Father, I ask for Your forgiveness for the ways I have allowed pride, ego, or a haughty Spirit to mask my insecurities. I recognize that true confidence does not come from exalting myself, but from humbling myself before You, *Spirit to Spirit*. Help me to see that authentic humility is not weakness, but strength. Remind me that my worth is not measured by the opinions of others, by fleeting achievements, or by outward appearances, but by my identity as Your beloved child, fearfully and wonderfully made.

Holy Spirit, guide me on my Spiritual Journey toward healing and restoration. Illuminate the hidden thirsts and hungers within me that have driven me to seek validation outside of Your Divine Will. Teach me to find contentment in Your Divine Presence, to embrace the unique gifts and talents You have placed within me, and to steward them for Your glory. Give me the courage to face the wounds of my past, to forgive myself of my shortcomings, and to release the pain of comparison and envy that has at times gripped my heart or plagued my mind.

Lord, I surrender my ego, my need for recognition, and my desire to please others at the expense of my own well-being. Replace my insecurities with the confidence that comes from knowing that I am accepted and loved by You. Grant me the discipline to govern my words, thoughts, actions, and reactions, so that I may reflect the character of Christ in all I do, say, and become. Help me to encourage others, to lift them up, and to walk in kindness, compassion, and grace, as one who knows their worth in You.

Father, I pray for discernment to recognize the difference between genuine humility and false modesty. Lead me away from the traps of comparison, coveting, and self-depreciation. Strengthen my Spirit so that I may resist the temptation to define myself by the standards of this world. Remind me daily that You have called me to a higher purpose, and that my true identity is rooted in Christ Jesus.

I ask that You heal every place in my heart where low self-esteem has left its mark. Renew my mind with Your truth. Restore my soul with Your love. Teach me to praise You for how fearfully and wonderfully I am made, and to believe, without wavering, that Your works in me are marvelous. May I always remember that my worth is not diminished by my past or by the judgments of others, but is eternally secured by Your Divine Grace and Mercy.

Thank You, Lord, for never giving up on me and for calling me out of darkness into Your marvelous light. I choose to rise above the labels and limitations that have been placed upon me. I choose to walk in freedom, confidence, and purpose, knowing that I am Yours. In Jesus' Name I pray, Amen.

PRAYER OVERRIDE 51

The Mark of Lukewarmness

Heavenly Father, I come to You with humility and honesty, recognizing the mark of lukewarmness that can subtly take root in my life. Lord, You see the depths of my Mind, Body, Soul, and Spirit, and I cannot hide from You. Even when I have settled for mediocrity or allowed complacency to guide my steps, You were in the midst of it. I confess that I have sometimes given You half of my heart, offering surface-level devotion instead of the passionate commitment You deserve.

Father, I acknowledge that You are not pleased when I go through the motions without true dedication to Your Kingdom. Forgive me for every moment I have treated You as a convenience or expected Your blessings for minimal effort. Forgive me for any time I have placed my desires or comfort above Spiritual Obedience, and for the times I have ignored the conviction of the Holy Spirit. I ask for Your Divine Mercy for every instance when I have rationalized sin, withheld forgiveness, or prioritized material things over matters of the Kingdom, including feeding Your precious sheep.

Holy Spirit, awaken within me a hunger and thirst for righteousness. Stir up in me a deep longing to know You, to serve You, and to walk in the fullness of my Divine Calling in accordance with my Predestined Blueprinted Purpose. In moving forward in the Spirit of Excellence, I pray that my prayers would become a joy rather than a chore, my worship would be wholehearted, and my time in Your Word would be precious and fruitful. Help me to seek You not out of obligation, but from a place of genuine love and gratitude, *As It Pleases You.*

Lord Jesus, shine Your Divine Light on every place in my life where I have become indifferent or disengaged. Reveal to me the habits, distractions, and attitudes that crowd out my time with You. Give me the courage to face the truth about my Spiritual State and the willingness to change. Teach me to recognize when I am operating in lukewarmness, and grant me the grace to repent and return to You with a fervent Spirit.

Father, strengthen my determination to pursue You above all else. When I am weary, fill me with Your strength. When I am tempted to coast through life or settle for less, remind me of the high calling You have set before me. Fill me with wisdom, not just knowledge, so that I may understand and apply Your truth in every area of my life. Help me to redirect any negative energy into positive action, using my Spiritual Gifts, Talents, and Creativity for Your Everlasting Glory.

Holy Spirit, move within me so that my faith will not plateau or stall, but grow stronger every day. Help me to serve others with joy, to extend forgiveness freely, and to be sensitive to the needs of those around me. Give me a Spirit of Excellence, so that I may honor You in all I do, say, and become.

Thank You, Lord, for loving me even in my seasons of lukewarmness. Thank You for Your patience and for calling me to a deeper, more vibrant relationship with You. I choose today to rise up, to speak life over myself, and to pursue You with all that I am. May my life become a reflection of Your Divine Love, Power, and Grace, for I know that with You, I can win and fulfill my Predestined Purpose, *As It Pleases You.* In Jesus' Name I pray, Amen.

Dr. Y. Bur

www.DrYBur.com

PRAYER OVERRIDE 52

The Mark of Lust

Heavenly Father, I come before You acknowledging the weight and danger of *The Mark of Lust*. Lord, You alone know the depths of my Mind, Body, Soul, and Spirit. I confess that I have not always guarded my heart as You have instructed. I recognize that lust is not limited to physical desire but often creeps into my thoughts, my ambitions, my eyes, and even my pursuit of status or recognition. I ask for Your forgiveness for every moment I allowed the desires of my flesh, the desires of my eyes, or the pride of life to overshadow my Spiritual Calling and Divine Purpose in You, *As It Pleases You*.

Father, I thank You for allowing my Spirit to belong to You, as I am reserved by Divine Design. Lord, I also thank You for allowing the Holy Spirit to be my Spiritual Guide, Comforter, and Teacher while allowing the Blood of Jesus to cover me as Spiritual Atonement. Above all, I am reminded daily in Earthen Vessel that my body is a Temple of the Holy Spirit, bought at the highest price, and that I am called to glorify You in all that I do, say, and become for my Heaven on Earth Experiences. Help me to honor this sacred trust, to reject anything that would lure me out of alignment with Your Divine Will, and to remain steadfast in my commitment to purity and righteousness.

Holy Spirit, awaken within me a deeper understanding of the boundaries You have set for my good. Strengthen my resolve to walk in self-control and discernment. Reveal to me any area of my life that has become a hiding place for lust, whether it appears as overindulgence, coveting, jealousy, pride, or the pursuit of things that do not please You. Give me the courage to confront, confess, and surrender these strongholds at Your feet.

Lord, I acknowledge that the valley of dry bones is a symbol of what happens when lust, envy, and pride drain my hope and leave me feeling lifeless. Breathe new life into me and restore what has been lost to overindulgence or misplaced desires. Where I have allowed my soul to become scattered or my purpose to become clouded, bring clarity, restoration, and renewal.

Father, teach me to walk in the Spirit, to cultivate gratitude and contentment, and to find fulfillment in Your Divine Purpose, according to my Predestined Blueprint. Help me to recognize the red flags or Spiritual Nudges when I am being pulled away by temptation or when my desires do not align with Your Divine Will. Guard my eyes, my thoughts, and my heart from every form of coveting, comparison, and idolatry. May I always remember that true satisfaction and joy are found in You alone.

Lord, grant me humility, the wisdom to choose the positive character traits that PLEASE You, and the strength to resist the lies and mind games of the enemy. Let my life be marked by kindness, gentleness, and authentic love, not by the empty pursuits of the world. I pray for the courage to stand firm in my authority as Your child, to bind and cast out every Spirit that is not of You, and to enforce my Spiritual Rights with boldness, as You have commanded.

I appreciate Your patience, for Your restoring power, and for the promise that no situation is beyond Your ability to redeem. I choose to surrender every lustful desire, every prideful thought, and every covetous ambition, laying them down at Your altar. Fill me with Your Spirit, renew my mind, and let my life bring glory and honor to You. In Jesus' Name I pray, Amen.

PRAYER OVERRIDE 53

The Mark of Mind Games

Heavenly Father, I come before You with a heart searching for truth, wisdom, and the courage to walk in righteousness, especially in the face of the mind games that surround me in this world. Lord, You know every hidden motive, every whispered thought, and every intention of my heart and mind. Your Word declares that You are a just Judge, that You search the heart and test the mind, and that nothing is hidden from Your sight. I acknowledge, Father, that if I dare to play mind games with others, I am truly playing myself. For You, O God, see past every clever word, every mask, and every scheme.

I ask You, Lord, to protect my heart and mind from the fiery darts of manipulation, deceit, and pride. Help me to guard my heart with all diligence, for I know that out of it flow the issues of life. Let my mind be renewed by the washing of Your Word, and may the Spirit of Truth guide my thoughts, actions, and intentions. Teach me to walk in wisdom, to be as wise as a serpent but as innocent as a dove, never using my intellect to harm or to deceive, but to uplift and to serve.

Father, when I am tempted to play games with the hearts and minds of others, remind me of Your Divine Justice and Your Everlasting Mercy. I know beyond a shadow of a doubt that You weigh every heart and mind and that there is a harvest for every seed sown, whether in secret or in the open. Let me not become a pawn in my own schemes, but instead, let me walk humbly before You, seeking to honor You in every interaction, every relationship, and every word spoken.

I confess, Lord, that this land, both within me and around me, is in desperate need of healing. I see the brokenness, the division, the pain, and the confusion that mind games and manipulation have caused. I see how the fruit of our lives is affected by the condition of our hearts and minds. Father, I ask You to heal the land within me. Uproot every seed of bitterness, envy, hatred, and pride. Plant in me, instead, the Fruit of the Spirit: Love, Joy,

Peace, Patience, Kindness, Goodness, Faithfulness, Gentleness, and Self-Control.

Lord, help me to be an example of healing, to become the illustration of restoration for those around me. Let the healing You begin in me overflow into my family, my community, and my nation. May my Body, Mind, Soul, and Spirit come into alignment with Your design, that I might honor You in all things. Show me how to respect and care for my body, as it is intricately connected to the land from which I was formed. Let the choices I make reflect gratitude for Your Divine Creation and a commitment to stewarding Your Spiritual Gifts well, *As It Pleases You.*

When I see hatred, division, and corruption in the world, help me not to respond with despair or more hatred, but with a resolve to sow love, hope, and truth. Remind me that true victory comes not through manipulation or control, but through humility, self-control, fasting, repentance, and prayer. Strengthen my will to turn away from my wicked ways, to humble myself before You, and to seek Your face with all my heart.

Father, Your Word promises that if Your people who are called by Your name will humble themselves, pray, seek Your face, and turn from their wicked ways, then You will hear from Heaven, forgive our sins, and heal our land. I take this PROMISE personally and commit to doing my part in this healing process. Heal me, Lord, that I may be an agent of healing in the land. Renew my mind, restore my Spirit, and revive my Inner-Born Purpose, that I may live a life that glorifies You.

I ask for discernment and wisdom to recognize the games the enemy plays and the courage to stand firm in truth and love. Help me to play my hand close to my chest, not out of fear or with a cunning demeanor, but out of a desire to walk in integrity and to honor You above all else. Let me not be overtaken by the mind control germ that seeks to break my unity and peace, but instead, fill me with the power and presence of the Holy Spirit, that I may stand victorious, unshaken, and steadfast in faith.

May my actions, words, thoughts, and intentions reflect the heart and mind of Christ. In addition, my Lord, may I become a Divine Vessel of peace, a bearer of hope, and a Spiritual Ambassador of Healing in a world desperate for Your touch. In Jesus' Name I pray, Amen.

PRAYER OVERRIDE 54

The Mark of Mind Reading

Gracious and Most Holy Father, I come before You with a heart full of humility and awe, knowing that You alone are the Searcher of hearts and the Knower of all thoughts. I acknowledge that before You, all things are laid bare, and nothing is hidden from Your sight. Lord, I confess that there are times when I have presumed to know the hearts and intentions of others, when in truth, only You possesses the authority and wisdom to discern the inner workings of the mind. Forgive me for every moment I have allowed myself to step into territory that is Yours alone, for the mind is sacred ground where You commune with each soul in the quietness of reflection and conviction.

Father, I recognize that within the body of Believers, there is a subtle temptation to believe that we can read the thoughts or intentions of those around us, especially when shared doctrines, traditions, and culture surround us. I see how easy it is to fall into patterns of assumption, to interpret another's mindset without dialogue, and to draw conclusions based on bias or group dynamics. Lord, deliver me from the pride that leads me to think I know what is in another person's heart, and protect me from the error of acting on these assumptions. Remind me that Spiritual Discernment is a Divine Gift, never a tool for unjust judgment, and never a substitute for genuine relationship or compassionate communication.

God, You have taught us to judge not by outward appearance, for You alone look upon the heart. Help me to remember that I am called to observe actions, to listen carefully to words, and to exercise wise judgment in love, but never to cross the sacred boundary into another's mind without invitation. Guard my heart against the sin of bearing false witness, of spreading assumptions as truth, and of damaging the reputation or dignity of another. When I am tempted to speak on what I do not know, let the Spirit of Truth restrain my lips and guide me into humility.

Holy Spirit, search me and know my heart. Reveal to me my own thoughts, whether they are positive or negative, right or wrong, just or unjust. Let me be quick to examine myself before I ever presume to examine another. Where my understanding is lacking, give me the wisdom to ask clarifying questions, to seek dialogue, and to honor the individuality of those around me. Teach me to value communication over conjecture, relationship over rumor, and grace over judgment.

Lord, I ask that You protect the minds of Your people. Let every Believer recognize the sacredness of the mind and conscience, and the danger of violating another's inner world. May we never trespass on Holy Ground by assuming what only You can know. If ever I become the victim of character assassination or false assumptions about my thoughts, give me the strength to stand firm in my Godly character and to trust that You are my vindicator. And if I am ever tempted to do the same to another, convict me deeply and draw me back to the path of righteousness.

Father, help me to be like Jesus, who, though He discerned the thoughts of men, always followed up with questions, inviting honest communication and repentance. Let me not fall into *The Mark of Mind Reading*, but rather pursue the Mark of True Understanding grounded in love, respect, and truth. Let my character and mindset be ever PLEASING to You, reflecting the uprightness and power that come from being filled with Your Spirit.

And so, I surrender my mind, my words, and my judgments to You. Purify my thoughts, sanctify my discernment, and let my life bear witness to the humility and grace of Christ. May I always seek to build up rather than tear down, to clarify rather than assume, and to honor the sacredness of every mind You have created. In Jesus' Name I pray, Amen.

PRAYER OVERRIDE 55

The Mark of Miscommunication

Heavenly Father, Most Gracious and Wise God, I come before You with a heart that longs to grow in the art of communication as You have intended it. I acknowledge that communication is a precious gift, a reflection of Your Divine Nature, and the very seat of who I am, as an Earthen Vessel, formed by Your hands. I thank You for granting me the ability to speak, to listen, to share ideas and emotions, and to build relationships through the power of words. Lord, I recognize that miscommunication is a subtle but devastating force that can divide, confuse, and wound. I confess that I have sometimes allowed misunderstanding, pride, and carelessness to cloud my delivery, forgetting that every word I speak carries the weight of my witness for Christ.

Father, Your Word teaches that the tongue holds the power of life and death. I ask You to make my tongue an instrument of healing, clarity, and unity. Teach me to choose my words with intention and to season them with grace, as Your servant Paul exhorted in Colossians. Let my speech be uplifting, edifying, and always rooted in love, never abusive or corrupt. Help me to remember that the Word of God is living and powerful, sharper than any two-edged sword, and that my delivery should honor its sacredness rather than stir up division or strife.

Holy Spirit, illuminate my mind and heart so that I may discern when anger, defensiveness, or offensiveness tries to creep into my communication. Replace those negative attributes with the Spirit of Lovingkindness, Patience, and Gentleness. Let kindness be the hallmark of how I deliver every truth, whether it is a word of correction or encouragement. Help me to slow down and listen, to speak from a place of calm and humility, and to remember that Spiritual Digestion takes time, just as the body needs time to process a nourishing meal.

Lord, give me the wisdom to know when to speak and when to be silent. Let my heart be free from the urge to win arguments or to appear superior, for it is not about who is right or wrong, but about honoring You in every exchange. Teach me to communicate with intention, sincerity, and a willingness to engage deeply with You and with others. Remove any selfish agenda or desire to violate the free will of those around me.

Father, I pray for a renewed mind, guarded thoughts, and a humble Spirit. Help me to forgive quickly, to repent earnestly, and to cover every word with the Blood of Jesus. Let me become one with the Holy Spirit so that my words and actions reflect Your Divine Guidance and Supernatural Wisdom. May my life and my message always be covered in gratitude, humility, and obedience. Let me serve others with joy and remain steadfast in trust for Your Divine Plan.

Lord, I desire to communicate in a way that makes the Spirit leap within those who hear me. Let my presentation be a reflection of my commitment to Spiritual Maturity, self-examination, and love. Fill me with patience, mercy, and accountability so that I may act and speak in a manner PLEASING to You.

Train my mouth to speak gracious words, as Ecclesiastes teaches, and keep me from the foolishness that swallows up wisdom. May my words always build up, inspire, and draw others closer to You. Let me be reminded daily that I must place the Holy Trinity first, pray, repent, forgive, fast, and seek unity with You, *Spirit to Spirit*. Help me to guard my thoughts, reverse negativity, remain humble, and use the Fruits of the Spirit in every interaction.

Father, I surrender my communication to Your refining fire. Shape my words, my tone, and my intentions until they MIRROR the heart of Christ. May every conversation be an opportunity for Your love and truth to illuminate the hearts of those I encounter. Let me never settle for empty words, but strive for impact that produces lasting Spiritual Growth, *As It Pleases You*. In Jesus' Name I pray, Amen.

PRAYER OVERRIDE 56

The Mark of Misguidance

Almighty and Everlasting Father, I come before You with a heart that trembles at the reality of misguidance in a world thick with deception. You are the God of Truth, the One who never changes, and whose Word stands forever. I acknowledge that in my own strength and understanding, I am prone to error, easily led astray by what seems right in my own eyes. Lord, I confess my vulnerability to the subtle snares of *The Mark of Misguidance*, and I humbly ask You to search my heart and purify my motives.

Father, Your Word declares that there is a way that appears right to a person, but its end is destruction. Shield me from the arrogance of thinking I always know what is right. Open my eyes to the ways that I may have been deceived, knowingly or unknowingly. Teach me to TEST the Spirit, to weigh the fruit, and to hold every teaching, every word, and every motive up to the light of Your truth. Let me never become so confident in my own knowledge that I neglect to seek Your Divine Wisdom and guidance daily.

Holy Spirit, I invite You to be my constant Teacher and Guide. Refine my discernment so that I am not swayed by empty words, persuasive arguments, or the appearance of light that conceals darkness. Give me a heightened awareness to recognize when someone or something is not aligned with Your Divine Will. When grace is present, let me feel its warmth and see its light, and when deception tries to creep in, alert my conscience with undeniable red flags to stand firm, *As It Pleases You.*

Lord, I pray for the humility to return to the Spiritual Classroom whenever I miss the mark or stumble. I do not want to lose even one of Your precious sheep to *The Mark of Misguidance* or error. Help me to embrace correction, to seek Spiritual Refreshment, and to value the Divine Covering of Your Everlasting Grace above all opinions or circumstances. Let me learn from the story of Job, who, despite trials and the voices of misunderstanding, clung to Your Divine Sovereignty and TRUSTED in Your ability to restore him when the time was right.

Father, I ask You to remove every influence, relationship, or situation in my life that does not contribute to the positive flow of Your Divine Grace and Mercy. If I have lost my covering or fallen short, grant me the strength to fast, pray, repent, forgive, and obey. Restore my Spiritual Sight so that I may discern the difference between what is good and what only appears good. Do not allow me to call evil good or good evil, but anchor me in the certainty that the Holy Spirit never misses the mark and never gets it wrong.

God of Grace, let Your Divine Illumination light up my life and the lives of those around me. May my words, actions, and beliefs always guide rather than misguide, and may I move forward with a heart fully surrendered to Your refining process. Keep me under Your covering, shielded from the wiles of the enemy, and positioned to fulfill Your Divine Purpose while feeding Your precious sheep with clarity, humility, and unwavering faith.

I surrender every truth I have trusted, every belief I have held, and every story I have told to Your examination. Expose all falsehood and replace it with Your PURE WISDOM. Let grace refine me, align me with Your Word, and empower me to respond, *As It Pleases You.* In Jesus' Name I pray, Amen.

PRAYER OVERRIDE 57

The Mark of Muteness

Sovereign and All-Wise Father, I come before You with a heart laid open, seeking Your Divine Presence, Your Everlasting Guidance, and Your Undeniable Truth as I confront the weight of muteness in my life. Lord, I know that silence is not always golden, for sometimes it is a sign of struggle, confusion, or even disobedience. Yet, I acknowledge that there are times when You, in Your Infinite Wisdom, hold my tongue or silence my voice for reasons that are HOLY and GOOD. I surrender both my speech and my silence to Your Divine Authority and ask for Your Spirit to lead me through the mystery of *The Mark of Muteness*.

Father, I confess that there are secrets and burdens that remain locked behind my lips, not always by my choosing, but sometimes by Your Divine Intervention. I realize that if my thoughts were to be laid bare, I would hang my head in shame, for You know every hidden motive and conceived thought, even those I have never acted upon. I ask You to purify my mind and heart so that what remains within me is PLEASING in Your Divine Eye. Let me not be defeated from the inside out by unspoken negativity, festering thoughts, or the toxic influences that sometimes go uncorrected in the quiet places of my psyche.

Holy Spirit, teach me to govern my thoughts, to bring every argument and high thing into captivity to the obedience of Christ. Help me to meditate on what is true, noble, just, pure, lovely, and of good report, as Your Word instructs. Grant me discernment to know when my silence is required for humility, reflection, or attentiveness, and when it is time to speak with boldness, clarity, and love. Search me, O God, and know my heart; try me, and know my anxieties; and see if there is any wicked way in me. Lead me in the way everlasting, breaking every chain of muteness that does not serve Your Divine Purpose in my life.

Lord, in times when I cannot hear Your Heavenly Voice, remind me to be still and attentive, to revisit Your previous instructions, and to wait upon You with patient expectation. Remove any Spiritual Wax that blocks my hearing, and make my ears sensitive to the gentle whispers of Your Spirit. If ever I find myself tempted to make up words or pretend to speak for You, convict me deeply and keep me from the silent rebellion of misrepresenting Your Divine Will. May I be quick to document, reflect, and repeat back to You what I believe I have heard, so that You may correct my understanding and bring me into GREATER ALIGNMENT with Your truth.

Father, empower me to break free from the prison of unhealthy silence, to overcome the tendency to ignore or downplay what needs to be said, and to refuse the burden of secrets that fester in darkness. Help me to become a conduit of Your Divine Wisdom, speaking only what You have called me to speak, and embracing silence only when You require it. Let my words and my quietness both be instruments of edification, healing, and peace in the lives of those around me.

Lord, I acknowledge that I will not get it right all the time, but I choose to align what I hear, say, do, and utter with the Word of God. I desire to walk in the Spirit of Righteousness, to behave Christlike, and to grow wiser with each passing day. Make me an Earthen Vessel of Your praise, a recipient of Your Divine Revelation, and a Faithful Steward of every word You entrust to me. In Jesus' Name I pray, Amen.

PRAYER OVERRIDE 58

The Mark of Neediness

Gracious and Providential Father, I come before You acknowledging my need for You above all else. Lord, I confess that there have been times when my heart has been overtaken by neediness, when my desires have clouded my vision, and when desperation has distorted my trust. I recognize that *The Mark of Neediness* is not simply about longing for more, but about losing sight of Your sufficiency and becoming entangled in my own expectations. I ask for Your forgiveness and for the strength to realign my soul with the abundance of Your Divine Grace.

Father, You have shown throughout Your Word that chasing after validation, fulfillment, or breakthroughs apart from You leads only to disappointment and Spiritual Famine. When I am tempted to seek validation from others, to compare myself, or to measure my worth by external things, remind me that my true identity is found in You alone. Help me to examine my motivations, my heart posture, and my deepest needs with honesty and humility. Let me never violate the free will of others or substitute my selfish ambitions for Your Divine Will.

Holy Spirit, teach me to recognize the subtle signs of neediness in my life. Search me and reveal any area where I am seeking to fill a void that only You can satisfy. If I am praying for personal gain rather than Your Predestined Purpose, shift my desires. If I am fearful of abandonment, increase my trust in Your abiding presence. If I am relying on possessions, achievements, or the approval of others for self-worth, gently turn my heart back to Your promises. Make me content in all circumstances, whether in abundance or in lack, knowing that You are my Jehovah Jireh, the Lord who PROVIDES.

Lord, help me to surrender control, to rest in Your Divine Timing, and to resist the urge to manipulate outcomes. Give me the courage to let go of guilt, shame, and the victim mentality, and to embrace gratitude, humility, and obedience. When I am anxious about the future or tempted to complain, remind me of Your Everlasting Faithfulness through every season. Let my love for others be genuine, not transactional or self-seeking, and let my service be a reflection of Your Divine Love.

Father, I ask that You break every cycle of neediness that keeps me from walking in freedom and fullness. Cover me with Your Spirit, and help me to operate in the Fruits of the Spirit, especially with self-control, patience, and peace. When Spiritual Challenges arise, give me the discernment and boldness to stand firm, knowing that You are greater than any opposition I may face. Let my life declare Your sufficiency, and may my TESTIMONY point others to Your Unfailing Provisions.

Lord, I choose to focus on Your Divine Abundance instead of my lack. I trust that You will provide in every area of my life, be it Spiritual, emotional, mental, relational, financial, and physical. Help me to fix my eyes on You, to remember Your faithfulness in the wilderness, and to walk forward in confidence and hope, regardless of my circumstances.

I surrender my needs, my desires, and my future to Your loving hands. Transform my heart so that I seek first Your Heavenly Kingdom and Your Unfailing Righteousness, trusting that all else will be added in Your perfect way. May I never be consumed by *The Mark of Neediness*, but instead be marked by faith, gratitude, and unwavering reliance on You. In Jesus' Name I pray, Amen.

PRAYER OVERRIDE 59

The Mark of Neglect

Merciful and Loving Father, I come before You carrying the weight of wounds both seen and unseen, asking for Your healing and restoration where *The Mark of Neglect* has left its imprint upon my life. Lord, I confess that there have been moments when I have felt overlooked, abandoned, or misunderstood, and at times I have been the one to overlook or neglect the needs of others. I recognize that neglect is a silent thorn, often woven deeply into the fabric of my experiences, and I ask You to reveal its presence, whether hidden in my heart, my actions, my thoughts, my words, or my relationships.

Father, I acknowledge that the scars of neglect can run deep, shaping my sense of worth, my relationships, and even my connection to You. I thank You that You see every wound, every tear, and every moment of rejection. I thank You that Your grace is sufficient, that Your strength is made perfect in my weakness, and that in my most broken places, Your love draws near to bind up my wounds. Help me to find comfort in Your Divine Presence and to rest in the assurance that I am never beyond Your attentive care.

Holy Spirit, search me and know my heart. Expose any area where I have neglected others, whether through my thoughts, words, actions, or the silence that fails to affirm, encourage, or support. Grant me the humility to acknowledge my shortcomings and the courage to make things right. Empower me to be attentive to those around me, to listen with empathy, to respond with kindness, and to show genuine care in both small and significant ways. Let my life reflect the love and compassion of Christ, who never fails to notice the overlooked or forgotten.

Lord, I ask for healing from the wounds of neglect, both those I have suffered and those I have inflicted. Where shame or isolation has taken root, uproot these burdens and replace them with the truth of my value and identity in You. Restore my heart so that I may love freely, forgive deeply, and extend grace to others as You have so freely given to me. Help me to recognize the triggers of past neglect and to respond with wisdom, patience, and self-control, rather than bitterness or withdrawal.

Father, I pray for Spiritual Discernment to recognize when I am drifting into patterns of neglect, whether through busyness, distraction, or self-protection. Teach me to pause, to examine my motives, to realign my heart with Your Divine Will, and to seek forgiveness where I have fallen short. Instill within me the discipline to follow through on my commitments, to honor my relationships, and to be present with those You have entrusted to my care.

Lord, may I never be content with simply avoiding harm, but strive to actively build up, encourage, and bless others. Let me walk in the fullness of Christlike Character, choosing kindness, respect, and compassion even in the face of unkindness or rejection. Help me to maintain healthy boundaries, protecting my heart while remaining open to Your Divine Purpose and Everlasting Love.

I commit myself to regular self-examination, asking You to continually refine my motives, thoughts, and actions. Give me the humility to seek repentance and the boldness to walk in forgiveness. May my life bear witness to Your Divine Mercy, and may I never allow *The Mark of Neglect* to define who I am or cause me to treat others unrighteously or unkindly. In Jesus' Name I pray, Amen.

PRAYER OVERRIDE 60

The Mark of Overreacting

Heavenly Father, Sovereign and Just, I come before You with a heart longing for Your Divine Wisdom and Guidance as I confront *The Mark of Overreacting* in my life. Lord, I confess that there have been moments when I have let my emotions dictate my actions, when I have asked for things outside of Your Divine Will, or responded to situations in ways that did not reflect Your Heavenly Character. I recognize that overreacting can invite Spiritual Sleepiness, Spiritual Sluggishness, and even Spiritual Oppression into my life, separating me from Your Unfailing Presence and clouding my discernment. I ask for Your forgiveness and for the transforming power of Your Spirit to awaken me from every slumber and lead me into truth.

Father, help me to examine my thoughts, beliefs, and desires with honesty and courage. Where there is provocation or unhealed pain, grant me the strength to confront these issues head-on and bring them into the light of Your Word. Guard me against the temptation to pray for things that violate Your Divine Will or the free will of others. Teach me to count the cost before I act, to weigh my words and actions carefully, and to always seek Your approval above all else.

Holy Spirit, train my heart to discern the right doors to knock on and the right requests to bring before the Throne of Grace. Remove any Spiritual Blinders that prevent me from seeing clearly, and deliver me from the oppression of Deceptive Spirits. When disappointment or confusion arises, remind me that Your answers may be yes, no, wait, or go back to the drawing board. Give me the humility to accept Your timing and direction, knowing that You see the end from the beginning and that Your plans for me are always for my good.

Lord, if fasting, repentance, or prayer is needed to break through stubborn barriers or to remove compounded negativity, give me the discipline and resolve to do what is required. Let me not shy away from the work of self-examination, but embrace it as a path to freedom and Spiritual Maturity. Help me to exercise extreme caution regarding what or whom I come into agreement with, guarding my Mind, Body, Soul, and Spirit from every form of Spiritual Invasion.

Father, I surrender every selfish or wayward tendency that I have hidden, asking You to expose anything in me that is not PLEASING to You. Break every generational curse and close every open door that allows Spiritual Unrest to take root in my life or in my lineage. Fill me instead with the Fruits of the Spirit, equipping me to respond to every situation with patience, kindness, self-control, and Christlike Love.

Lord, I desire to be a doer of Your Word, not a hearer only. Let my life reflect the humility and obedience that PLEASES You, and give me the courage to face myself honestly in the mirror of Your truth. May my reactions be governed by Your Spirit, and may my heart remain steadfast in the assurance of Your Everlasting Love and Devout Faithfulness.

I trust that as I align my desires with Your Divine Will, You will provide the answers, guidance, and breakthroughs that I seek. Strengthen me to stand firm against provocation, to remain vigilant in prayer, and to always walk in the LIGHT of Your Divine Wisdom. In Jesus' Name I pray, Amen.

PRAYER OVERRIDE 61

The Mark of Paranoia

Almighty and Compassionate Father, I come before You acknowledging my vulnerability to *The Mark of Paranoia*, which at times clouds my mind and heart with fear, distrust, and uncertainty. Lord, I confess that there have been moments when I have allowed paranoia to dictate my thoughts, reactions, and decisions, rather than trusting in Your Divine Sovereignty and Surefire Love. I ask for Your forgiveness and Your help in transforming my paranoias into power, *As It Pleases You*, so I can walk in the freedom and peace You have PROMISED.

Father, I recognize that paranoia often springs from seeds of fear, unhealed trauma, disappointment, and the desire for control. I admit that I have sometimes denied these feelings, allowing them to fester and grow stronger in the shadows of my psyche. Help me to bring all my hidden worries, insecurities, and doubts into the light of Your truth. Teach me to break the cycles of negative thinking, to replace paranoia with pronoia, believing that You are working all things together for my good.

Holy Spirit, guide me to the place of metanoia, where my mind is transformed, my character is refined, and my outlook is made new by Your power. Instill in me a Spirit of Eunoia, so I may cultivate a positive mindset, see win-win possibilities, and respond to challenges with faith and hope. Reveal to me when I am slipping into patterns of dysnoia or hypernoia, and gently lead me back to the path of peace and sound thinking.

Lord, help me to confess and forsake any thought patterns or behaviors that are not PLEASING to You. Let Your Divine Mercy wash over my mind and restore me to a place of emotional and Spiritual Balance. Remind me that paranoia is not a sin, but that unchecked paranoia can lead me into darkness or the separation from You and my Predestined Blueprinted Purpose. Grant me the courage to seek healing for my wounds, to forgive those who have contributed to my fears, and to forgive myself for the times I have doubted Your Unfailing Faithfulness.

Father, I commit to becoming a work-in-progress, striving to become better, stronger, and wiser, *As It Pleases You*. I refuse to remain a prisoner to my fears and insecurities. Instead, I invite You into the deepest places of my heart, asking You to transform every fear into faith, every suspicion into trust, and every anxiety into rest. Let me find my security in Your Unchanging Love and the assurance that You are always with me.

Holy Spirit, empower me to engage my emotional self with honesty and humility, to ask the questions that lead to growth, and to embrace the lessons found in my struggles. Help me to understand and honor the Spiritual Laws and Principles taught by Jesus, so that my life may be a TESTIMONY to Your Divine Grace and Supernatural Power. Keep me from striving for false perfection, and instead, lead me in the way of continual learning, healing, serving, and transformation.

Lord, I surrender my need for control, my desire to predict every outcome, and my tendency to expect the worst. Fill me with faith, hope, and love, and let Your Perfect Love cast out every fear. May Your Spirit Supernaturally Guide me daily, restoring my mind, renewing my heart, and anchoring my soul in the truth of Your Foolproof Promises. In Jesus' Name I pray, Amen.

PRAYER OVERRIDE 62

The Mark of Perfection

Most Gracious and Perfect Father, I come before You acknowledging that only You are truly perfect and complete in all Your ways. Lord, I confess that I have sometimes pursued perfection according to my own standards, or have judged others and myself with unrealistic expectations. I recognize *The Mark of Perfection* as a subtle snare that can lead to pride, frustration, and self-righteousness. I ask for Your Unfailing Forgiveness and for the humility to embrace my imperfections, trusting that Your Divine Grace is sufficient for me.

Father, I admit that I am not flawless, nor am I meant to be. I make mistakes, I fall short, and I often see areas in my life that need growth and correction. Help me to leave room in my heart for learning, for repentance, and for transformation as I become a work-in-progress, *As It Pleases You*. Teach me to welcome Your loving discipline, knowing that it is a sign of Your care and commitment to my growth as Your beloved child.

Holy Spirit, search my heart and reveal any ways in which I have allowed perfectionism to control my thoughts, words, actions, or relationships. Deliver me from the need to appear flawless, to rely on my own strength, or to pretend that I have arrived. Instead, fill me with a Spirit of Excellence that seeks to honor You, not by striving for unattainable standards, but by surrendering daily to Your refining work within me.

Lord, grant me the humility to apologize when I am wrong, to ask for forgiveness, and to seek advice from others when needed. Help me to extend the same grace to others that I so desperately need myself, refusing to judge or compare, but choosing to encourage, uplift, and love, *As It Pleases You*.

Father, I thank You that my worth is not determined by my achievements or by measuring up to a human definition of perfection. My value rests in being Your child, redeemed by Christ and sustained by Your Spirit. Let my life reflect the Spirit of Excellence, Integrity, and Righteousness, not perfectionism. May I walk in humility, teachability, and openness, always willing to learn, to grow, sow, and to receive correction as a GIFT from the Heavenly of Heavens.

Lord, I surrender the burden of perfection and embrace the freedom of being fully known, fully loved, and continually transformed by You. Keep me from pride, self-righteousness, and harshness toward myself or others. Let my heart be soft, my mind open, and my Spirit willing to be shaped and molded by Your hands.

I choose to rest in Your Infallible Grace as I pursue excellence, *As It Pleases You*. My Heavenly Father, I trust that You are at work in me, completing what You have begun for my Heaven on Earth Experiences. May my imperfections be reminders of my need for You, and may my life bring GLORY to Your Name and the Kingdom, as I walk in HUMILITY and LOVE. In Jesus' Name I pray, Amen.

PRAYER OVERRIDE 63

The Mark of Perversion

Holy and Righteous Father, I come before You with a humble and honest heart, acknowledging that I am in need of Your Divine Cleansing and Redemptive Power. Lord, I confess that *The Mark of Perversion* has touched humanity in ways that are often hidden, downplayed, or misunderstood, including in my own life. I recognize that perversion is in turning aside or away from Your righteousness, goodness, love, and Divine Intent, whether it be in my thoughts, actions, motives, or desires. I ask for Your Divine Forgiveness and for the strength to walk in purity, truth, and integrity, *As It Pleases You*.

Father, I admit that perversion is not limited to the obvious or the external. It can be subtle, corrupting my moral compass, distorting my ethical, sexual, or Spiritual Conduct, and leading me into rebellion or idolatry. I recognize that in covering up, denying, or minimizing these issues, I only give them room to grow. I ask You to shine Your Divine Light into every hidden place within me, exposing every form of perversion so that it can be brought under the Blood of Jesus and contained by the POWER of Your Spirit.

Holy Spirit, search me and reveal where I have strayed from Your path. Break every chain of corruption, distortion, or negativity that seeks to warp my heart, my mind, my character, or my relationships. Give me the courage to face the truth about myself without shame or fear, knowing that Your Divine Grace is greater than my weakness. Help me to discern the difference between conviction and condemnation, choosing always to run toward Your mercy and never away from it.

Lord, I ask for Divine Wisdom and Vigilance to guard my mind, my heart, and my body from any influence or temptation that leads me astray. Teach me to recognize the ways in which perversion can manifest, in my words, my attitudes, my entertainment choices, my desires, and most of all, my

Spiritual Practices. Empower me to reject all that dishonors You and to pursue what is pure, noble, and PLEASING in Your sight.

Father, help me to walk in the Spirit of Integrity, Righteousness, and Holiness. Let my life be a Living TESTIMONY to Your transforming power. Remind me that past or present failures do not define me, but by Your Unwavering Love and by the new identity I receive through Christ Jesus. Give me the humility to confess when I have fallen short, and the boldness to seek help and accountability when needed.

Lord, I choose to surrender every rebellious or idolatrous tendency that competes with Your Lordship in my life. I lay down every form of perversion, whether secretly or openly, and ask You to sanctify me through and through. Protect me from any form of Spiritual Deception or Demarcation as You help me to cultivate a heart and mind sensitive to Your Steadfast Leading. May I never be content with partial obedience but strive for wholehearted devotion to You.

Holy Spirit, fill me afresh with Your Divine Presence, Wisdom, and Power. Guide me in the way everlasting and restore every place in my life that has been marred by perversion or compromise. Let my thoughts, words, and actions reflect the PURITY and HOLINESS of Christ.

I thank You, Father, that where sin abounds, grace abounds much more. I receive Your Constant Forgiveness, Your Unfailing Covering, and Your Supernatural Strength to overcome. Let my life be marked not by perversion, but by restoration, integrity, and love, so that others may see Your Unwavering Glory and be drawn to You. In Jesus' Name I pray, Amen.

PRAYER OVERRIDE 64

The Mark of Placement

Sovereign and All-Knowing Father, I come before You seeking clarity, humility, and alignment as I confront *The Mark of Placement* in my life. Lord, I confess that I have sometimes lost sight of my true belonging and position in You, searching for identity, acceptance, or influence in places that do not honor Your Divine Intent. I recognize that when my sense of placement is distorted, I am vulnerable to brokenness, confusion, and judgment. I ask for Your forgiveness and for the guidance of Your Spirit to keep me grounded in Your Undeniable Truth and Predestined Purpose.

Father, I acknowledge that the stories written in Your Word reveal the consequences of misplaced desires, actions, and relationships. I see how *The Mark of Placement* is not limited to one area, but can affect every part of my life, including my family, my relationships, my mind, and my community. When I allow my thoughts, emotions, or desires to drift from Your Divine Will, I open the door to chaos, confusion, and Spiritual Blindness, Deafness, or Muteness. Help me to recognize the signs of a debased mind, lukewarmness, dullness, or when being stiff-necked, and to quickly turn back to You whenever I am tempted to stray.

Holy Spirit, search my heart and reveal any area where I have resisted Your Divine Wisdom, rejected Your correction, or ignored my conscience. Expose every mindset, action, or attitude that is out of alignment with Your Word. Grant me the humility to admit when I am wrong, the courage to seek Your Unbiased Forgiveness, and the wisdom to realign myself with Your Divine Wisdom. Do not let me become desensitized to conviction or allow my conscience to be dulled by repeated carelessness.

Lord, I ask for strength to resist the pull of negative influences, and to discern the difference between right and wrong, good and evil, just and unjust. When I am tempted to act out of misplaced desires or to seek validation apart from You, remind me of my true identity as Your beloved child. Give me a mind that is sensitive to Your Principled Leading and a Spirit that is quick to obey, *As It Pleases You.*

Father, protect me from the dangers of moral confusion and Spiritual Blindness, safeguarding the VISION needed for my Heaven on Earth Experiences. Keep my conscience tender, my thoughts pure, and my actions aligned with Your Divine Will. When I fall short, help me to repent quickly and to receive Your Divine Grace with gratitude and humility. Teach me to seek placement only in You, trusting that You alone determine my worth, my purpose, and my destiny.

Holy Spirit, fill me with wisdom and discernment, so that my life may reflect Your order, peace, and righteousness. Let my relationships, decisions, and pursuits honor You, bringing healing where there has been brokenness and restoration where there has been chaos. Guard me from the temptation to play a demigod in my own life or in the lives of others, and keep me humble in Your Divine Eye.

Lord, I surrender every misplaced desire, every rebellious thought, and every action that is not PLEASING to You. Place me exactly where I belong, under the covering of Your Undeniable Grace and in the center of Your Divine Will. Let my life be a TESTIMONY to Your faithfulness, and may I never settle for anything less than Your Divine Placement, *As It Pleases You.* In Jesus' Name I pray, Amen.

PRAYER OVERRIDE 65

The Mark of Player Hating

Righteous and Loving Father, I come before You with a heart searching for humility and freedom from *The Mark of Player Hating*. Lord, I confess that there have been moments when I have harbored envy, jealousy, or resentment toward the success, gifts, or blessings of others. I admit that insecurity and pride have sometimes shaped my words, thoughts, or actions, leading me to criticize, undermine, or withhold kindness from those whom You have chosen to elevate. I ask for Your forgiveness and the cleansing of my heart, so that I may walk in the Spirit of Love, Encouragement, and Unity.

Father, I recognize that player-hating is born from a Spirit of Comparison and a lack of gratitude for what You have given me. I do not want to be someone who resents or criticizes others, nor do I want to stand by and remain silent when I should offer a loving warning or a helping hand. Remind me that every person is uniquely crafted by Your Divine Hand and that their successes do not diminish my own worth, Spiritual Calling, or Divine Blueprint.

Holy Spirit, search my heart for any sign of bitterness, competitiveness, or ill will. Where I have failed to celebrate others or have spoken or acted out of envy, convict me and lead me to repentance. Help me to root out any negative character traits that cause division, isolation, or harm, and replace them with good fruit that honors You and builds up Your precious sheep. Teach me to wish others well, even if their path looks different from mine, and to rejoice in their victories as I trust You with my own journey.

Lord, give me the courage to restore others in a Spirit of Gentleness when they have fallen, to bear their burdens, and to seek their good above my own pride. Let me never withhold an opportunity for someone to grow, learn, or be restored because of my own issues. Help me to remember that my calling is to lead by example, to love without conditions, and to serve with humility, not to judge, ostracize, or play god in anyone's life.

Father, I thank You for the many second chances You have given me, for the battles You have fought on my behalf, and for the wisdom You have poured into me through every season. Let my story be a TESTIMONY of Your Divine Grace, Everlasting Mercy, and Transforming Power. May I use every blessing, lesson, and opportunity not to boast or compare, but to BLESS and LIFT UP others as You have done for me.

Holy Spirit, align my mind and heart with Your Divine Will. Remove every trace of player hating, and fill me with a Spirit of Affirmation, Compassion, and Genuine Joy for others. Let my character and fruit reflect Christlikeness, and may my actions always point others back to Your Unfailing Love and Your Unadulterated Truth. In Jesus' Name I pray, Amen.

PRAYER OVERRIDE 66

The Mark of Playing God

Almighty and Sovereign Father, I come before You with a humbled heart, recognizing that only You possess the Divine Authority, Wisdom, and Power to rule all things. Lord, I confess that there have been times when I have tried to seize control, to pass judgment, or to direct the fate of others, forgetting my need to seek Your Divine Guidance, *As It Pleases You*, and to walk in humility. I acknowledge *The Mark of Playing God* as a dangerous temptation that lurks in small and subtle ways, luring me to trust more in myself than in You.

Father, I repent for every moment of self-idolatry, pride, or arrogance that has led me to elevate my will, my desires, or my opinions above Yours. Forgive me for the times when I have made decisions without regard for others, when I have overlooked their feelings, or have failed to consider the wisdom of counsel and the importance of humility. Expose every root of self-importance, covetousness, or desire for status in my heart, and cleanse me with Your Unbiased Truth.

Holy Spirit, reveal to me any area where I have become blind to my own flaws and errors. Grant me the courage to face myself honestly, to surrender my need for control, and to lay down every tendency to play god over my life or the lives of others. Teach me to walk in humility, recognizing that I am not the judge, but a servant called to lead with compassion, wisdom, and grace.

Lord, keep me from the path of becoming Your enemy through arrogance, self-righteousness, or friendship with the world. Remind me daily that exaltation and promotion come from You alone, and that my true worth is found in obedience and surrender to Your Divine Will. Help me to seek connection with You, *Spirit to Spirit*, so that my discernment remains clear and unclouded by my selfish motives.

Father, I ask for the grace to reverse negativity with a positive Spirit, to counteract pride with humility, and to meet every temptation to play god with the power of submission and trust. Let me learn to lead and serve as Jesus did, always pointing others back to You and never seeking glory for myself. Guard my heart from self-deception, and fill me with the courage to admit when I am wrong, to seek forgiveness, and to restore what has been damaged by my own actions, words, beliefs, or desires.

Holy Spirit, empower me to walk in the Law of Spiritual Duality, to use the authority You have given me for good and not for harm. Let my leadership reflect Your Divine Love, Justice, and Truth. May I always remember that the changing of guards and the shifting of seasons are in Your hands alone, and that I am simply a steward of all that You entrust to me.

Lord, I surrender every area of my life where I have played god, knowingly or unknowingly. Place me under Your Divine Covering, and let my life be marked by humility, faith, and obedience. May I lead, serve, and love in a way that honors You and draws others closer to Your heart. In Jesus' Name I pray, Amen.

PRAYER OVERRIDE 67

The Mark of Poverty

Heavenly Father, Gracious Provider, I come before You acknowledging that every good and perfect gift comes from Your Heavenly Hand. Lord, I confess that I have sometimes struggled with *The Mark of Poverty*, whether in my mindset, my Spirit, or my circumstances. I recognize that poverty is not just about material lack, but an inward blindness, deafness, and muteness that can keep me from SEEING and RECEIVING Your Divine Abundance.

Father, I realize that when I focus on scarcity, limitations, and what I do not have, I risk missing the blessings, opportunities, and Divine Movements You have placed all around me. Forgive me for any moments when I have allowed negativity, comparison, or ungratefulness to cloud my vision. Help me to break free from every lie, stigma, or expectation that tries to define my worth by worldly standards, knowing that my true value rests in being Your beloved child.

Holy Spirit, search my heart for any residue of a poverty mindset, fear of lack, or inward agreement with mediocrity. Uproot every seed of insecurity, envy, or hypocrisy that would keep me from walking in my Predestined Purpose with Christlike Character Traits and outright humility, *As It Pleases You*. Teach me to see myself and others through the eyes of grace, wisdom, and possibility. Give me the courage to pursue my Divine Calling boldly, to develop my Spiritual Gifts, and to serve with a grateful and generous Spirit. Lord, I thank You for the lessons learned through my seasons of lack, rejection, or disappointment. I see now that faithfulness is not always measured by outward reward, but by a heart anchored in trust and obedience to You. Strengthen my resolve to seek Your Kingdom and righteousness first, believing that all other things shall be added according to Your Divine Will.

Father, grant me discernment to recognize and reject the shadows of pretense and hypocrisy, whether in myself or in the systems around me. Help me to value integrity and honesty above appearances, to honor You with my thoughts, my words, my actions, and my stewardship. Let my relationships, ambitions, and contributions be rooted in authenticity, not in striving for approval or recognition.

Holy Spirit, fill me with the Spirit of Gratitude, Contentment, and Creativity. Restore my vision to see the hidden wealth within myself, within others, and within every opportunity You provide. Empower me to lead, bless, and build beyond myself, leaving a legacy of faith, hope, and love for generations to come.

Lord, I choose today to break the agreement with *The Mark of Poverty* and to embrace my identity as a child of ABUNDANCE, called to reflect Your generosity. May my life be a TESTIMONY of Your faithfulness, and may I walk forward with confidence, creativity, and courage, regardless of the circumstances I face. In Jesus' Name I pray, Amen.

PRAYER OVERRIDE 68

The Mark of Pretense

Heavenly Father, Giver of Truth and Authenticity, I come before You with a heart seeking to be free from *The Mark of Pretense*. Lord, I confess that there have been times when I have worn masks, played roles, or hidden my true self behind a veil of appearances. I acknowledge that pretense, whether born of fear, insecurity, or a longing to belong, cannot withstand the heat of Your refining presence. I ask for Your forgiveness and for the courage to step into the light of authenticity, embracing who I am in You.

Father, I realize that pretending may serve as a temporary shield, but it ultimately distances me from genuine connection, healing, and purpose. I do not want to be unusable in Your Kingdom by being fake, nor do I want to forfeit my Divine Covering by operating outside the Spirit of Excellence. Teach me the wisdom of humility, the beauty of vulnerability, and the strength that comes from depending on Your Supernatural Power instead of my own.

Holy Spirit, search my heart and reveal any desire for attention, validation, or control that is not rooted in truth. Show me where I have allowed pride, comparison, or fear of rejection to govern my actions or interactions. Help me to see myself and others through You, with compassion and understanding, so that I may esteem others above myself, as Your Word instructs.

Lord, protect me from the pitfalls of pretense. When I am tempted to put on a show or hide my weaknesses, remind me that the enemy seeks to exploit my vulnerabilities, but You use them to shape my character and draw me closer to You. Let me not be swayed by fleeting validation, toxic relationships, or the intoxication of the spotlight. Keep my heart anchored in authenticity, my mind guarded by humility, and my Spirit led by Your truth.

Father, grant me discernment to recognize pretense in myself and in others, not for the sake of judgment, but to foster honest and meaningful connections. Teach me to ask open-ended questions, to listen without bias, and to respond with KINDNESS and GRACE. Help me to navigate challenging relationships with wisdom, choosing dialogue over debate, and understanding over assumption.

Holy Spirit, fill me with the Spirit of Excellence and the courage to stand firm in my true identity, even when it is uncomfortable. Let my words, actions, and intentions reflect Christlike humility, so that others may see Your Undeniable Love and Supernatural Power at work in me. Guard me from pride, self-deception, and the need to perform, and lead me into a life of transparent service and genuine love.

Lord, I surrender every mask, every false persona, and every need to pretend. I choose to walk in the freedom and light of authenticity, trusting that You will lift me up in due season, and that true greatness is found in humility, service, and love. May my life be a TESTIMONY to Your Transformative Grace and a beacon for others seeking to break free from *The Mark of Pretense*. In Jesus' Name I pray, Amen.

Dr. Y. Bur

www.DrYBur.com

PRAYER OVERRIDE 69

The Mark of Pride

Mighty and All-Seeing Father, I come before You with a heart humbled by the weight of *The Mark of Pride*. Lord, I confess that pride has at times crept into my words, my ambitions, and my relationships, disguising itself as confidence or zeal, while quietly drawing me away from humility and dependence on You. Forgive me for the moments when I have sought my own glory, craved attention, or judged others by appearances instead of by the FRUIT of their character.

Father, I acknowledge that pride is a subtle but powerful force, capable of deceiving even the most well-intentioned hearts. I recognize that the enemy uses pride to turn leaders and followers alike away from the path of righteousness, causing division, confusion, and harm in the Body of Christ. Guard me from the dangers of prideful ambition, self-promotion, and the temptation to justify unrighteousness for personal gain.

Holy Spirit, search the depths of my heart and expose every motive that is not PLEASING to You. Reveal any hidden arrogance, envy, or desire for control that may be shaping my actions or attitudes. Help me to walk in true humility, to seek Your Divine Approval above all else, and to serve others with a Spirit of Gentleness, Kindness, and Love. Remind me that the Fruits of the Spirit: love, joy, peace, patience, kindness, goodness, faithfulness, gentleness, and self-control, are the true marks of a life surrendered to You.

Lord, I ask for Divine Discernment to recognize false prophets, deceptive leaders, and wolves in sheep's clothing. Give me the Supernatural Wisdom to TEST the Spirits, to measure every teaching against the truth of Your Word, and to be vigilant in guarding my heart and mind from prideful influences. Where I have been complicit in pride, whether by condoning it or by failing to stand for truth, grant me the courage to repent and to realign with Your Divine Will.

Father, keep me from becoming a tool of deception or division, and instead, make me a vessel of humility, accountability, and sincere devotion. Let my leadership and influence be marked by a servant's heart, always pointing others to Christ and never to myself. Help me to honor Your flock, to care for Your people, and to protect the integrity of the Body of Christ.

Holy Spirit, empower me to confront the wolf within, to resist the urge to hide behind a façade, and to nurture a heart that is authentic and pure. Let me never be content with outward displays of righteousness while neglecting the hidden places of my psyche. Teach me to be quick to repent, eager to forgive, and steadfast in pursuing the path of humility, even when the world rewards pride and self-promotion.

Lord, I thank You that You see all things, know all motives, and will bring every hidden thing to light. Keep my focus fixed on glorifying You, not myself. May my life, my words, and my actions be a TESTIMONY to Your Undeniable Truth, Your Righteous Justice, and Your Irrefutable Mercy. Let me always remember that it is better to serve in humility than to reign in pride. In Jesus' Name I pray, Amen.

Dr. Y. Bur

www.DrYBur.com

PRAYER OVERRIDE 70

The Mark of Ramifications

Heavenly Father, Almighty God, I come before You with a humbled heart, seeking Your Divine Wisdom and Guidance as I contemplate *The Mark of Ramifications*. Lord, You know all things, and nothing escapes Your Precise Eyesight. You see the intentions behind my actions, my thoughts, my beliefs, and my desires. I ask You to search me and reveal anything within me that does not align with Your Divine Will. Help me to rightly discern the consequences of my choices, to understand not only what I do, but why I do it, and why I often hesitate to do what I know is right.

Father, I acknowledge that every decision I make sets into motion a ripple effect that reaches far beyond myself. Let the Holy Spirit guide my steps so that the outcomes of my life bring glory to Your Name and blessings to those around me. If there are places in my life where I have been silent or inactive, forgive me and awaken a holy boldness within me. Speak to me through my Spiritual Language, in ways that I can understand, for the level I am on. Remove fear, confusion, and pride from my heart, and replace them with clarity, humility, and a readiness to obey.

Lord, I invite the Holy Spirit to speak to me and through me. Let my Spiritual Language be more than words or utterances, but a living connection to Your Presence. Open my ears to hear Your Heavenly Voice, whether it comes as a whisper, a word, or a sign. Let me never limit the ways in which You choose to communicate with me. Help me to recognize the marks and consequences of my actions, to own my mistakes, and to respond in repentance and faith. Remind me that You are a God of order and purpose, and that nothing happens by chance.

God, I ask for the fullness of the GIFTS of the Spirit, not for my own gain, but that I might serve as a vessel fit for Your use and to feed Your precious sheep, *As It Pleases You*. Help me to use wisdom, knowledge, faith, healing, miracles, discernment, tongues, and interpretation, always under the

GUIDANCE of the Spirit and in alignment with Your Word. Shield me from deception, pride, and the Spirit of Nimrod that seeks to build apart from You. May I never attempt to outdo Your Divine Wisdom or walk in arrogance, but always submit to Your Loving Authority with outright humility.

Father, I repent for every time I have tried to build my own tower, for every moment I have acted apart from Your Divine Directions or Blueprint. Tear down anything in me that is not founded upon Your Heavenly Truths. Let my life be built on Christ Jesus, the solid rock, and let my words, actions, and desires bear witness to Your Unwavering Love and Supernatural Power. Guard my Mind, Body, Soul, and Spirit from *The Mark of Ramifications*, and set a watch over my heart so that I may not be led astray.

Holy Spirit, fill me afresh. Use my Spiritual Language to edify, to heal, to restore, and to unite. Teach me to recognize Your Spiritual Voice above all others, and to be obedient no matter the cost. Where I am weak, make me strong. Where I am uncertain, give me faith. Where I am discouraged, fill me with hope. Use me to speak life into my dry bones, use me to bring light to dark places, and use me to reflect Your Divine Glory in all that I do.

Lord, I surrender every ramification of my past, present, and future to You. Redeem what has been broken, restore what has been lost, and reveal Your Divine Purpose in every outcome. Let my life be a TESTIMONY of Your Loving Grace and a beacon of hope for others. In Jesus' Name I pray, Amen.

PRAYER OVERRIDE 71

The Mark of Recklessness

Heavenly Father, my Righteous Judge and Protector, I come before You with awe and humility, seeking Your Divine Wisdom as I reflect on *The Mark of Recklessness* as revealed through the story of Dinah. Lord, You alone see the depths of my heart and the hidden corners of my intentions. As I consider the weighty lessons of Genesis 34, I ask You to search my Mind, Body, and Soul, and remove any Spirit of Recklessness, haste, or vengeance that may try to take root within me.

God, I acknowledge that curiosity and impulsiveness can sometimes lead me into places I am not prepared to enter. I confess that I have sometimes rushed forward without Your Divine Counsel, trusting in my own strength rather than leaning on Your Spirit. At times, I have also failed to do my homework, ventured where I should have paused, and neglected the wisdom of waiting upon You. Forgive me for the times I have acted in haste, for every decision I have made that brought unnecessary pain or risk to myself, to others, and most of all, to the Kingdom.

Father, I ask for the Spirit of Wisdom to guide my every step. Let me not be led by unchecked emotions or the pressure of others, but by the gentle guidance of Your Spirit. Remind me that true strength is found in self-control, that justice belongs to You, and that vengeance is Yours alone. When I am tempted to react in anger or respond in deceit, hold my tongue and steady my hands. Let me not become the very thing I despise by repaying evil with evil or violence with violence.

Lord, I lift up to You every place in my life where I have allowed *The Mark of Recklessness* to stain my conscience. Cleanse me, purify my motives, and help me to address my unresolved pain and my known or unknown difficult issues with openness and honesty. Grant me the courage to protect the vulnerable, the discernment to recognize danger, and the humility to seek reconciliation where there has been harm. May I never violate another's dignity or innocence, but instead protect and honor those entrusted to my care.

Heavenly Father, help me to foster open communication within my family and community, so that misunderstandings and secret grievances do not fester or explode in destructive ways. Let my actions be governed by love, patience, and respect for boundaries. Teach me to regulate my emotions, to forgive quickly, and to pursue healing after trauma. When I am faced with situations that test my integrity, let me choose to walk in the Spirit and not in the flesh.

God, I pray that Your Divine Wisdom would sanctify my curiosity, that Your Spiritual Protection would cover my ventures, and that my relationships would be marked by peace and honor. Help me to stay in the lane You have prepared for me, to resist the temptation to cross boundaries that are not meant for me, and to trust Your timing in all things. Let me not invite regret by acting rashly or unprepared, but instead move forward under the covering of Your Spirit.

Lord, I surrender my desire for revenge, my tendency toward rash decisions, and my inclination to justify wrongdoing. Help me to remember that every choice carries consequences, and that I am called to be a Divine Vessel of Your grace and not an instrument of destruction. May I never lose Your Divine Favor through reckless living, but instead grow in wisdom, understanding, and self-control.

Father, shield me from *The Mark of Recklessness* that leads to ruin, and fill me instead with the Spirit of Wisdom, Counsel, and Understanding. Let my life be a reflection of Your Justified Justice and Timely Mercy, and may I always choose forgiveness and healing over bitterness and retaliation. May I be known as a peacemaker, a protector, and a restorer.

In all things, I seek Your Supernatural Guidance, Your Heavenly Presence, and Your Bountiful Blessings. Cover my loved ones and me with Your protection as we *Override the Marks of the Beast* and walk in the fullness of Your Spirit. In Jesus' Name I pray, Amen.

PRAYER OVERRIDE 72

The Mark of Regret

Heavenly Father, I come before You with a heart both heavy and hopeful, reflecting on *The Mark of Regret* and the lessons it holds. Lord, You know my deepest thoughts and the moments in my life when I have grieved over missed opportunities, broken relationships, unspoken words, and actions taken without wisdom. I confess my regrets before You, knowing that nothing is hidden from You. I invite Your Holy Spirit to shine light into these places within me, to reveal what I must learn, and to transform my regret into a wellspring of growth and understanding, *As It Pleases You.*

Father, I pray for the courage to face my regrets honestly. Help me to see them not as chains that bind me, but as stepping stones leading me closer to Your Divine Will. Let me not cause others regret, but rather be a Divine Vessel of encouragement and healing. Where I have erred, grant me humility to seek forgiveness and make amends. Where regret has settled in my Spirit, let Your grace uproot its bitterness, replacing it with hope and wisdom.

Lord, teach me how to reverse engineer the element of regret, to analyze its origin and recognize the patterns that led me astray. May Your Spirit grant me discernment to recognize the nudges that come from You. Help me to distinguish between the whispers of Your Spirit, the urgings of my own heart, the influence of others, and the schemes of the adversary. Let my heart be ever attentive to Your Supernatural Guidance, so that I may awaken my Creative Baby and allow it to leap at Your prompting.

Father, I thank You for the Spiritual Gifts, Talents, and Callings You have placed within me. I pray for fresh creativity to be stirred from within, for the Child of Creativity in me to rise up and play, to explore, and to build as You lead. Where my GENIUS has governed with caution, loosen its grip so that the Spirit of Creativity may flow freely for Your Eternal Glory. Remove the mask of regret that the enemy would have me wear and reveal the Divine Creativity You have ordained for my life.

Lord, I ask for the humility to learn from every regretful moment, for the strength to move beyond shame, and for the faith to trust in Your Redemptive Power. May I capture every idea, no matter how small, and submit it to Your Refining Wisdom. Let my creativity not be stifled by fear of failure or past disappointments, but let it be ignited by the hope of what You can do with a surrendered heart.

Help me, Father, to possess the trust of a child, to rely on You as my loving Parent, and to rest in the assurance that You make all things new. Let the characteristics of Jesus be formed in me, so that I may not bear *The Mark of Rejection*. But instead, reflect the mark of Your Present Grace, Manifesting Love, and Unbiased Acceptance.

Above all, my Lord, I surrender my regrets, my creativity, and my very life into Your hands. I ask that You would use every part of my Spiritual Journey for Your Kingdom and Your glory. In Jesus' Name I pray, Amen.

PRAYER OVERRIDE 73

The Mark of Rejection

Heavenly Father, I come before You with a heart laid bare, humbled by the wounds and lessons that come with rejection. Lord, You know the sting I have felt, the deep ache of being overlooked or misunderstood, and the moments I have, in my own frailty, rejected others. You see every sorrow and scar, every time I have turned away from those You love, sometimes believing it sets me apart for the better. I confess my shortcomings, asking You to cleanse me from every attitude or action that does not reflect Your Unfailing Love and Deepest Compassion.

Father, I thank You that rejection is never wasted in Your hands. You take what the world tosses aside and transform it into something beautiful. I acknowledge that my disappointments are not dead ends; they are stepping stones for Your Divine Purpose. I ask that You would open my eyes to see every moment of rejection not as a sentence, but as an opportunity for growth, healing, and breakthrough. Mold my heart so that I do not harbor bitterness or resentment, but instead, allow Your Spirit to reverse every *Mark of Rejection* into a Cornerstone of Greatness, *As It Pleases You.*

Lord, I surrender my Creative Spiritual Gifts, my Inner Genius, my Creative Baby, and every hidden part of myself to You. Wash away the debris and contamination that the world brings, even when I do not see it coming. Purify my motives, cleanse my intentions, and restore my soul so that Your Spirit may rest upon everything I offer, whether it is my talents, my callings, or my daily actions. Help me to be honest with myself, to recognize when I am adapting to Spiritual Filth or Compromise, and give me the courage to seek Your Divine Cleansing from the Heavenly of Heavens.

Father, I ask for a right Spirit within me; a Spirit that seeks reconciliation and restoration with others, that reaches out instead of withdrawing, that builds bridges instead of walls. Teach me to treat others with the same grace You have shown to me. Help me to see that the way I treat others is a reflection of how I view myself and my relationship with You. Where I have harbored pride, envy, or judgment, forgive me. Where I have withdrawn love, compassion, or encouragement, renew my heart so I may overflow with the Fruits of Your Spirit, *As It Pleases You.*

Lord, I ask for wisdom to rightly divide truth, to discern my purpose, and to walk in the fullness of my Spiritual Identity, according to my Predestined Blueprinted Purpose. Let me not be hindered by the marks of the past, nor by the opinions of others. I thank You for the Hidden Trinity within me: My Spirit, my Soul, and my Character that are fashioned in Your Image, waiting to be UNVEILED by You. Therefore, in my waiting, preparing, and learning phases, may I draw nearer to You, so that my Genius is connected to Your Holy Spirit, Your breath inspires my creativity, and the example of Jesus Christ shapes my character.

Where I have been tempted to pursue material things or fleeting comforts, realign my heart to pursue righteousness and excellence in all that I do, with integrity and compassion. Teach me to serve others selflessly, to give without expectation, to comfort the hurting, and to lift those who are weighed down by their own burdens. Let my life be a TESTIMONY of Your grace, a platform that encourages others to rise, to leap with joy, and to discover their God-Given Purpose as You have done or are doing for me.

Father, help me to learn from every obstacle, to extract wisdom from every trial, and to share freely from the overflow of Your Abundant Blessings. Let me not be selfish with my Spiritual Gifts or stingy with my encouragement. Instead, may I always have one hand reaching up to You and one hand reaching back to help others, creating a rhythm of grace and generosity in my life while feeding Your precious sheep, *As It Pleases You.*

Thank You, Lord, that I am not defined by rejection, but by redemption. Thank You for securing me by the Blood of Jesus and for empowering me through Your Spirit. May my Creative Baby leap for joy, not only for my sake, but for the sake of all whom You have called me to SERVE and INSPIRE. I Spiritually Seal this prayer with GRATITUDE and SURRENDER. In Jesus' Name I pray, Amen.

PRAYER OVERRIDE 74

The Mark of Resentment

Heavenly Father, I come before You today acknowledging the heaviness that *The Mark of Resentment* has pressed upon my soul. I confess that at times I have allowed bitterness, anger, and unrighteousness to wrap around me like grave clothes, keeping me bound in places You have called me to be free. Lord, I know that if I refuse to see resentment for what it is, I cannot remove these grave clothes, and I will remain hindered from walking in the fullness of the new life You have given me.

Father, I ask for Your Divine Intervention to help me recognize every layer of Spiritual Stench that resentment brings into my life, the life of others, and the Kingdom. I surrender every known and unknown trigger that has caused bitterness to take root in my heart. I realize that the longer I ignore or downplay these wounds, the more deeply they bind me and the harder it becomes to break free without Your help. You alone, Lord, can bring me out of this invisible chokehold and place me on the path of freedom and healing.

Lord, just as Jesus removed His grave clothes and set them aside by folding them neatly. I also ask You to help me lay aside every weight of resentment and put things in their proper place. Help me to understand that nothing that has happened in my life is without purpose. If You have allowed it, then there is value to be found. Give me the wisdom to extract the lesson from every trial with a work-in-progress mindset, and the grace to move forward with dignity, forgiveness, and in the Spirit of Excellence.

Father, I acknowledge the thorns in my flesh, the persistent difficulties and afflictions that keep me humble and reliant on You, *Spirit to Spirit*. I thank You for loving me enough not to let me become puffed up or self-sufficient. Help me to see that even my weaknesses and struggles have a role in Your Divine Plan, and that Your strength is perfected in my weakness.

Lord, I confess that at times I have been triggered by others, by circumstances, and even by the fear of losing control. I have been tempted to blame others or hold grudges, forgetting that these responses only hold me captive. I ask You to renew my mind and teach me to redirect the energy of my triggers toward positive growth and understanding. Let me see my triggers as opportunities to exercise wisdom, develop self-control, and create win-win situations that reflect Your Divine Love and Unbiased Truth.

Father, give me the courage to pause when I am provoked, to breathe deeply, and to seek Your Supernatural Guidance before I react. Remind me to take a step back, to pray, to reflect, and to regain my balance before making decisions or speaking words that may wound others or myself. Help me to govern my thoughts and emotions so that they serve Your Divine Purpose and feed Your sheep, rather than becoming weapons of destruction.

Lord, help me to become a Triggered Genius, fully aware of what moves me, what stirs me, and what brings out the best in me. Let me answer honestly the questions that reveal my heart, so that I may turn every trigger into a source of wisdom and creativity, rather than pain and regret. Show me how to look within and seek resolution through Your Spirit before searching for answers outside of myself.

Father, I ask that You would fill me with the Fruits of the Spirit: Love, Joy, Peace, Patience, Kindness, Goodness, Faithfulness, Gentleness, and Self-Control. Let these qualities abound in me, replacing every trace of resentment and bitterness. Make my life a TESTIMONY of Transformation, so that I may encourage others to seek freedom from their own grave clothes. Let me be a Vessel of Grace, always willing to forgive, always eager to learn, and always ready to love as You have loved me.

Thank You, Lord, for Your Longstanding Patience and Revered Mercy. Thank You for the freedom that comes from surrender and the healing that comes from Your Healing Touch. I receive Your cleansing today and declare that the mark of resentment has no lasting power over me. I step out of the tomb of bitterness and into the light of Your purpose, ready to live and love with a renewed Spirit. In Jesus' Name I pray, Amen.

PRAYER OVERRIDE 75

The Mark of Rotten Fruit

Heavenly Father, I come before You with a heart seeking Your Divine Light, humbled by the truth that from the Garden of Eden until now, the battle has always been about the FRUIT I bear. Lord, I recognize that the desire for wisdom and pleasure outside of Your Divine Will can mark me with the stain of rotten fruit, making me a liability in Your Kingdom rather than an asset. I confess that at times I have allowed my words, my thoughts, and my actions to reflect spoiled fruit, born of wounds, neglect, or selfishness rather than the pure and life-giving Spirit You intended for me.

Father, I thank You for Your everlasting grace and mercy, which sustain me even when I have not recognized the mark upon me. Yet I do not want to remain asleep or numbed by my own shortcomings. Awaken me, Lord, to the reality of my fruit and the impact it has on my relationship with You, with others, and even within myself. Reveal to me the triggers, seeds, and roots that have caused my fruit to spoil, and grant me the discernment to see beyond my surface symptoms to the seed of the problem within my heart.

Lord, help me to examine my life with honesty and humility. Let me not shy away from the difficult questions about my actions, my words, and my motives. Grant me the courage to repent and forgive, to pray and fast, and to release every offense and burden to You. Where I can change, give me the strength to make the adjustments You require. Where I cannot change, help me to surrender and trust in Your Perfect Wisdom and Timeless Treasures.

Father, fill me with the desire to bear good fruit worthy of repentance. Let the fruit of my mouth, my thoughts, and my deeds be PLEASING in Your sight and a blessing to those around me. Teach me that my fruits are not for selfish consumption, but for the building up of others, for the protection of my soul, and for the advancement of Your Kingdom. May I give love if I desire love, offer joy if I seek joy, extend peace if I need peace, and sow kindness, goodness, faithfulness, gentleness, and self-control as a free-will offering, knowing that in due season I will reap a harvest according to the Law of Reciprocity.

Lord, help me to reject bad fruits and influences without shame or fear, standing firm in my God-Given right to guard my Tree of Life, *As It Pleases You*. I am also reminded that You have already provided the Spiritual Roadmap I need for my Blueprinted Journey. Let me meditate on Your word day and night so that I may be like a tree planted by the rivers of water, bearing fruit in due season, with leaves that do not wither, and prospering in all that I do, say, and become.

Father, I ask for Your Divine Wisdom and Abounding Grace as I train the next generation. May I raise my children and influence those around me with the fear of God, in integrity, and through the Fruits of the Spirit. Let me be a good steward, never provoking but nurturing and admonishing in love, so that their character is molded to reflect Your Divine Light rather than the darkness of this world.

Lord, I desire to break every negative cycle and avoid consuming my own fruit out of selfishness or rebellion. In doing so, renew and rejuvenate my Mind, Body, Soul, and Spirit. At the same time, grant me the understanding, growth, and regrafting needed to move forward in the Spirit of Excellence with Divine Power, Authority, Unity, and Interconnection, *As It Pleases You*. Let me walk in obedience, not rebellion, knowing that in surrendering to Your Divine Will, I will find true FREEDOM and JOY.

Father, I renounce every mark of rotten fruit in my life. Cleanse me, restore me, and empower me by Your Spirit to walk as a new creation. Let my obedience open the Divine Pathway for my Heaven on Earth Experiences, as my life TESTIFIES to Your Redemptive Power.

As the Creator of all things, I offer all that I am and all that I have to You, my Heavenly Father. I am trusting and abiding in You to bear much fruit. Yes, Lord, the Spiritual Fruit that remains, the Spiritual Fruit that brings GLORY to Your Heavenly Name with no shame attached. In Jesus' Name I pray, Amen.

PRAYER OVERRIDE 76

The Mark of Self-Gratification

Heavenly Father, I come before You with a humble heart, seeking Your mercy and grace as I confront *The Mark of Self-Gratification* in my life. I confess that at times, I have allowed my selfish desires and fleeting pleasures to cloud my sense of good judgment and distance me from Your Perfect Will. My Lord, forgive me for every moment or situation when I have chosen my own way over Yours, placing my wants above righteousness and obedience to Your Word and Ways. I acknowledge that true fulfillment is found only in the total surrender to Your Divine Purpose and Blueprinted Plan for my life.

Lord, I thank You for the Spiritual Tools and Ammunition that You have graciously provided. You have given me prayer, fasting, repentance, forgiveness, meditation, and the infallible Word of God. I thank You for the Fruits of the Spirit, Christlike Character Traits, gratefulness, the guidance of the Holy Spirit, the cleansing power of the Blood of Jesus, and my Spiritual Armor full of truthfulness, humility, and obedience. In addition, I am also grateful for Your Supernatural Authenticity, Foolproof Righteousness, Spiritual Gifts, Divine Creativity, and the Predestined Blueprint You have placed within me, allowing me to TAP INTO them, *As It Pleases You*. In doing so, I rejoice in faith, hope, love, courage, resilience, compassion, empathy, kindness, and a commitment to lifelong learning. For You have indeed pre-equipped me with everything I need to walk in Spiritual Victory, even amid seeming defeat.

Father, I ask that You teach me how to MASTER the use of these Spiritual Gifts and Tools, not for my own glory, but *As It Pleases You*. Help me to discern the enemy, whether within me, around me, or lurking unseen, and to stand firm against every attack. Let me never use my Spiritual Gifts for manipulation, personal gain, or to elevate myself above others. Remove any trace of a mean-spirited heart or a desire to control, intimidate, or shame

Your people. Purify my motives, O God, so that I may walk in humility and serve as a Divine Vessel of Your Free-Flowing Love and Compassion.

Help me to recognize and reject the temptation to gratify myself at the expense of others. Guard my heart against the lure of materialism, status, and fleeting pleasures. Empower me to build both the visible church and Your Kingdom within me. May I invest my resources, time, and talents into the Divine Blueprint You have PREORDAINED for my life. Give me the courage to break every word curse, whether spoken over me or by me, and teach my tongue to speak only what is good, edifying, and full of grace. Let no corrupt word proceed from my mouth, but only those that impart grace and life.

Lord, help me to see the value in every person, never treating anyone as less than or using them for my advancement. Give me wisdom to discern the patterns of manipulation and exploitation around me and the strength to stand apart from a culture that exploits and devalues others. May I honor the dignity You have placed in every soul and refuse to participate in any form of exploitation, knowing that all of us are created in Your Image.

Father, I pray for the Body of Christ. Let us break every chain of selfishness, greed, and Spiritual Dullness, Lukewarmness, or Stiff-Neckedness. Restore us to a place of Holy Reverence and Authentic Love for one another. Raise up Leaders and Believers who walk in Your Spirit, who value integrity and truth, and who are not swayed by personal ambition. Let us be known for our compassion, generosity, and unwavering commitment to Your Kingdom.

I thank You, Lord, for the intangible BLESSINGS that are freely given to me, such as life, love, grace, mercy, forgiveness, peace, joy, hope, wisdom, strength, salvation, compassion, faith, guidance, purpose, protection, provision, and the UNVEILING of Your Creation. Remind me daily that these are not to be earned or hoarded, but RECEIVED and SHARED with gratitude and humility. By Your Spirit, teach me to walk in freedom, to live generously, and to love unconditionally.

Today, I reject every word curse, every lie of the enemy, and every pattern of self-gratification that seeks to undermine my Divine Destiny or Spiritual Blueprint. I declare that my life is founded on Your Everlasting Truth and Purpose. I choose to walk in obedience, relying on the Supernatural Power of the Holy Spirit to sustain me. May my words and actions be PLEASING to You, and may my life bear the unique TESTIMONY to Your Transforming Grace. In Jesus' Name I pray, Amen.

PRAYER OVERRIDE 77

The Mark of Soul Ties

Heavenly Father, I come before You acknowledging the weight and reality of the known and unknown soul ties in my life. I confess that at times, I have connected myself to people, places, things, and situations that were not PLEASING to You. Plus, I have allowed my Mind, Body, Soul, and Spirit to become entangled in bonds that have drawn me away from Your Divine Purpose and Presence. I recognize that Spiritual Transfers are real, and I ask for Your Divine Wisdom and Discernment to purify my soul from every unrighteous tie.

Lord, I thank You for the GIFT of the Holy Spirit, who reveals Real Truth and Divinely Guides me on the Path of Holiness. I ask that You shine Your light into every hidden place within me. Expose every unhealthy soul tie that lingers in my Spirit, my emotions, my memories, or any hidden crevice of my psyche. Give me the courage to acknowledge these connections and the strength to release them, trusting that You have better for me than anything I have left behind.

Father, I repent for every moment when I allowed my emotions, desires, or loneliness to lead me into relationships or encounters that were not aligned with Your Divine Will. Forgive me for the times I have carelessly taken in the emotions and energy of others, allowing negative Spirits to take root within me, sift me, brainwash me, or outright manipulate me. Wash me with the Blood of Jesus, and cleanse every part of my being, Mind, Body, Soul, and Spirit, leaving no place untouched, *As It Pleases You.*

I ask You now to break every bond of bondage that has come from being unequally yoked. Where I have taken in emotions that do not belong to me, I ask that You uproot them from my soul. Where I have received energy that drains, depresses, or depletes me, I surrender it to You for healing and restoration. Replace every void with Your Perpetual Love and the fullness of the Holy Spirit.

Father, help me to recognize the patterns of unhealthy relationships and to discern when I am unequally yoked. Give me wisdom to see beyond superficial attraction, to value good character, and to honor the boundaries You have set for my protection. Let me not seek to change others for my benefit, but instead focus on my own growth and character development as You work in me.

Lord, I renounce every unhealthy attachment and soul tie. I forgive those who have hurt me, and I ask for Your grace to forgive myself for choices I regret. I cover every memory, every emotion, and every connection with the Blood of Jesus. I invite the Holy Spirit to fill every place within me that was once occupied by these ties, yokes, or strongholds. Guide me in letting go of or cutting the cord on every reminder that keeps me bound to the past.

As the Creator of all things, replace my thoughts with Your Divine Truth, getting rid of the lies as I am reminded of my identity in Christ Jesus. Lead me toward the relationships that honor You and contribute to my growth in faith and character. Help me to recognize the difference between godly bonds that build and ungodly ties that destroy.

Father, I declare that every soul tie related to my childhood, my behaviors, my sins, my wounds, my traumas, my fears, my words, my thoughts, and my relationships is broken right now, in the Name of Jesus. I speak freedom over my life, and I claim the promises of Your Word that those whom the Son sets free are free indeed.

Lord, strengthen my Spirit to stand firm against the lure of unrighteous associations, addictions, longings, untruths, and lusts. Help me to take control of my thoughts and to use positive affirmations grounded in Your Word. Let me walk in the power of the Holy Spirit, with a renewed mind and a heart set on PLEASING You.

I thank You for Your Present Grace, Eternal Mercy, and Unending Love. I thank You for the victory that is mine through Christ Jesus. Today, I choose to detach myself from every unrighteous soul tie and to embrace the FREEDOM and wholeness You have PROMISED me. In Jesus' Name I pray, Amen.

PRAYER OVERRIDE 78

The Mark of Stunted Growth

Heavenly Father, I come before You with an open heart, seeking Your Divine Wisdom and Guidance as I wrestle with *The Mark of Stunted Growth* in my life. Lord, I confess that there are times when I feel stuck and unsure of which way to turn. I admit that I have sometimes allowed the cares of this world and the distractions of material gain, status, and self-reliance to take precedence over the calling You have placed upon my life. Forgive me for those moments when I have chosen rebellion and disobedience, and for the times I have depended on others rather than stepping into the potential You have given me.

Father, I acknowledge that *The Mark of Stunted Growth* is not new, for it was present even in the Garden of Eden. I ask that You grant me the discernment to recognize when I am hindering my own Spiritual Growth and to resist the temptation to settle for less than what You have destined for me. Help me to break free from the inner conflicts, insecurities, and emptiness that arise when I fail to embrace my purpose. Lord, when I am disillusioned or confused, lead me back to Your Divine Presence, *Spirit to Spirit*. When fleeting desires and false expectations cloud my vision, remind me of the eternal values of Your Kingdom.

Holy Spirit, fill me afresh with the Fruits that come from Your Divine Presence: Love, Joy, Peace, Patience, Kindness, Goodness, Faithfulness, Gentleness, and Self-Control. May these Spiritual Virtues rise up within me and overflow into every aspect of my life. I desire to be transformed from the inside out, so that my character and attitude reflect the LIGHT of Christ and bring glory to Your Name. Teach me to listen to correction and embrace discipline, knowing that through Your loving direction, I will grow in understanding, favor, and wisdom.

Lord, help me to resist the urge to compare myself to others or to hide behind a mask of pretense. Strengthen me to overcome the urge to judge or to wound others with my words or actions. Let humility be the mark of my life, so that I may build others up and encourage them to discover the greatness You have placed within them.

Father, I surrender my self-imposed limitations to You. I ask for the courage to step out in faith and do the things You have called me to do, trusting that my Spiritual Gifts will make room for me in due season. With the help of Your Spirit, I choose to embrace wisdom, to seek understanding, and to love righteousness. May I always remember that lasting success comes not from my own striving, but from walking in obedience and faithfulness to You.

Lord, I thank You that Your faithfulness remains steadfast even when I struggle with doubt or unfaithfulness. Help me to dwell safely in Your Eternal Presence, secure and unafraid of evil, as I listen to Your Heavenly Voice and follow Your Divine Ways. I pray that You would continue to mold my character, renew my mind, and ignite a passion within me to fulfill my Divine Purpose. In Jesus' Name I pray, Amen.

Dr. Y. Bur

www.DrYBur.com

PRAYER OVERRIDE 79

The Mark of Struggling Sabotage

Heavenly Father, I come before You with humility and sincerity, acknowledging my struggle with sabotage in my life. Lord, I recognize that sometimes I am my own worst enemy, making choices that seem wise in my own eyes yet are not aligned with Your Divine Will. Forgive me for the times when I have depended on my own understanding or sought advice from others before seeking You. I confess that I have made decisions based on my desires and limited perspective, and at times, I have fallen out of step with the Purpose You have written for me.

Holy Spirit, open my eyes to the moments when I self-sabotage. Help me to discern when I am acting out of fear, pride, insecurity, or unresolved pain. Empower me to rebound from my mistakes and to self-correct as I walk this journey. Teach me to allow my failures and bad choices not to define me, but to REFINE me, as You have refined precious gold and silver. Remove any toxic impurities from my heart, so that I may be a Spiritual Vessel fit for Your Divine Service and worthy to feed Your precious sheep, *As It Pleases You.*

Lord, I ask for the courage to embrace my personal refining process, knowing that it is necessary for my growth and Spiritual Well-being. Protect me from the temptation to pretend or put on a show for others. Grant me the strength to admit when I am wrong and the wisdom to learn from every experience. Help me to guard my heart with all diligence, for I know that from it flow the issues of life.

Father, where there is unresolved trauma, bring Your Supernatural Healing. Where there is a tendency to destroy or harm, whether myself or others, replace it with a Spirit of Restoration and Peace. My Lord, from this moment forward, I choose to walk in the Spirit of Excellence, striving to represent Your Kingdom with Christlike Character Traits. Let the Fruits of the Spirit, Love, Joy, Peace, Patience, Kindness, Goodness, Faithfulness, Gentleness, and Self-control, be evident in my life and actions.

Holy Spirit, help me to refine my communication, time management, listening, conflict resolution, and every area that needs growth. Fill me with self-discipline and a desire to walk in integrity, no matter who is watching. Teach me to pay attention: to You, to myself, to my environment, to my strengths and weaknesses, and to the lessons You are teaching me. Enable me to forgive myself and others, to give thanks for the lessons sabotage has taught me, and to rise above every hindrance that would keep me from fulfilling my Divine Destiny.

Lord, I know that sabotage can come in many forms, such as self-sabotage, people-sabotage, environmental sabotage, and so on. Therefore, I ask that You reveal every hidden form of sabotage in my life while giving me discernment to recognize and overcome each one. When I am tempted to consume my own Spiritual Gifts or Fruits selfishly or to avoid humility, remind me of the calling to serve and to share with others.

Father, connect my Spirit with Your Holy Spirit, so that I may be awake and alert both physically and Spiritually. Grant me the grace to be vigilant, to hear and see what You reveal through my conscience, dreams, and visions, and to access the SECRETS of the Spirit. May I never fall into Spiritual Slumber, but remain Spiritually Alert, Sensitive, and Responsive to Your Supernatural Leading.

I thank You for the Spiritual Tools and Anointing You have made available to me, and I receive them with gratitude. Help me to walk in my Predestined Purpose, rebounding and self-correcting as You empower me, so that my life will reflect Your GLORY and bring HONOR to Your Name. In Jesus' Name I pray, Amen.

PRAYER OVERRIDE 80

The Mark of the Lone Ranger Syndrome

Heavenly Father, I come before You with gratitude for Your ever-present love and guidance. Lord, I confess that there are times when I fall into the trap of *The Mark of the Lone Ranger Syndrome*, believing that I am alone, that my struggles must be carried in solitude, and that asking for help is a sign of weakness. Forgive me, Father, for the pride and fear that keep me from reaching out to others and for forgetting that You never intended for me to walk this journey alone.

Holy Spirit, remind me daily that I am never truly alone. You, O God, as the Father, Son, and Holy Spirit, are always with me, surrounding me with Your Divine Presence, strengthening me in times of need, and guiding me along the path of righteousness. I thank You for the people You have placed in my life, those who are vessels of Your love, wisdom, and support. Grant me discernment to recognize when to seek help, along with the humility to accept it, trusting that You provide for me through the hands and hearts of others.

Lord, when I am tempted to isolate myself, help me to remember Isaiah 41:10, that I need not fear or be dismayed, for You are my God who promises to strengthen, help, and uphold me. Break the chains of loneliness and self-reliance that keep me from experiencing the fullness of You, *Spirit to Spirit*. Teach me to trust in Your Divine Providence, knowing that You make a way even when I face rejection or disappointment.

Father, I bring before You the hidden skeletons in my life, along with the secrets, regrets, and past mistakes that sometimes haunt me. I ask for the courage to repent, to forgive, and to bury these things under the cleansing power of the Blood of Jesus. Free me from the temptation to revisit the past and empower me to embrace the new life You have prepared for me. Help me to lay every burden on Your Divine Altar before seeking counsel from others, so that my healing and restoration come first from You.

Holy Spirit, deliver me from the Spirit of Childishness. Help me to put away immature thoughts, behaviors, and reactions, and to embrace the maturity You desire for me. Strengthen my resolve to walk as an adult in the faith, perfecting HOLINESS out of reverence for You. Let my inner child be a source of creativity and joy, guided by the WISDOM and DISCIPLINE of Your Spirit, rather than by my ungoverned emotions or wounds of the past.

Lord, help me in becoming and remaining mindful not to become selfish with the Spiritual Gifts, Wisdom, and Assignments You have given me. Let me be generous in sharing what I have, willing to serve others, and to help recover Your lost sheep. Fill me with compassion, patience, and humility, that I may be a reflection of Your Enduring Love to those around me.

Father, I ask that You help me to maintain healthy boundaries, to care for my own soul and household as I reach out to others. Guide me in seeking balance so that I do not neglect my own responsibilities while serving those in need. May I always seek to operate with integrity, discernment, and a pure heart.

I thank You for the Spiritual Tools and the BLESSING of Your Holy Spirit, who grants me basic wisdom, strength, and comfort until I am strong enough to handle the Divine. Help me to continually grow in Spiritual Awareness, so that I may recognize Your Sacred Voice and Your Foolproof Guidance in every season of my life.

Lord, I surrender my need for control and my fear of vulnerability to You. Teach me to walk in the freedom of knowing that I am never alone, for You are with me and You provide for me in ways beyond my understanding. May my life be a TESTIMONY to Your Profound Faithfulness and Undeniable Grace. In Jesus' Name I pray, Amen.

PRAYER OVERRIDE 81

The Mark of the Love of Money Maze

Heavenly Father, I come before You with a heart humbled by the lessons of the maze I find myself in. Lord, I confess that there have been times when I have wandered in circles, seeking fulfillment in material things, striving for success, or searching for a way out of my struggles by means other than Your Spirit. Forgive me for the moments when I have looked to money as a solution or allowed it to become an idol in my life. I acknowledge that the maze of the love of money can be subtle and deceptive, enticing me with promises of security and happiness that it cannot truly provide.

Holy Spirit, grant me Divine Wisdom to pay attention to where I have been and where I am going. Help me to see the signs and lessons along the path and to avoid the traps of materialism and distraction. Remind me that my true wealth is found in You and that the greatest treasures are those of the Spirit: Love, Joy, Peace, Patience, Kindness, Goodness, Faithfulness, Gentleness, and Self-Control. Keep my eyes fixed on the path You have set before me, that I may labor for my Divine Blessings with integrity and gratitude, not driven by greed or envy.

Lord, I ask that You help me to learn from every weakness and challenge, recognizing them as hidden blessings, opportunities to grow closer to You, and to share my TESTIMONY with others. When I find myself in a place of confusion or frustration, teach me to speak life to my dry bones, to cover my circumstances with Your Word, and to invite the Holy Spirit to fill every empty place within me. Give me the courage to rise quickly from despair and to walk boldly in the power You have given me.

Father, I thank You for the Spiritual Maze that refines my character and shapes my destiny. Help me to navigate it with humility, teachability, and a willingness to learn. May I never judge the journey of another, but focus on my own path, trusting that my will, empowered by Your Spirit, will lead me to Your intended purpose. Guard my heart against the temptation to violate the free will of others or to seek control where only surrender is required.

Lord, reveal to me the areas in my life where I have tried to fill longings or emptiness with money or possessions. Expose every soul-violation zone, and heal every place where my Spirit has been depleted. Teach me to value what money cannot buy, especially when it comes to love, peace, faith, and the joy of Your Divine Presence. If I am stuck in a psychological maze, grant me clarity and wisdom to find the way out through Your Spirit.

Holy Spirit, awaken my Spirit Man and teach me to trust Your Supernatural Guidance above my own understanding. Help me to relinquish control, surrendering every outcome to Your Perfect Will. Let my Spirit be one with Yours, moving in harmony with You, *Spirit to Spirit*, experiencing the supernatural peace and confidence that comes from TRUE UNITY with You.

Father, I pray for the discipline to follow the Trail of Wisdom, to exhibit the Fruits of the Spirit, to share my Spiritual Journey with others as a result of Your Beautiful Faithfulness, and to inspire others to seek You above all else.

I thank You for the Divine Creativity You have placed within me. Let it flourish as I walk according to Your Predestined Purpose, never losing sight of the true riches found in You. Strengthen my willpower to choose what is right, and keep my heart aligned with the Principled Values of Your Kingdom. In Jesus' Name I pray, Amen.

PRAYER OVERRIDE 82

The Mark of Thievery

Heavenly Father, I come before You with a humble heart, acknowledging the weight and truth of Your Word. Lord, I recognize that *The Mark of Thievery* is not only about the overt act of stealing but also about the subtle ways I may take from others, whether by action or attitude. It is underhanded theft, robbing others of their creativity, joy, and dignity. I confess, Father, that there have been times when I have taken advantage, whether by neglect, dishonesty, entitlement, or failing to honor the contributions of others. I see now that such ways disrupt trust, harm relationships, and stifle the gifts You have placed within each of us.

You have called me to a higher standard. Your Word in Ephesians 4:28 commands, *"Let him who stole steal no longer, but rather let him labor, working with his hands what is good, that he may have something to give him who has need."* Lord, I desire to move from being one who takes or uses others to one who gives and feeds, *As It Pleases You*. I do not want to operate in the Spirit of Ungratefulness, Forged Fakeness, nor do I want to leave behind any trace of selfishness or exploitation. I want to be known for generosity, for building others up, and for leaving a mark of selfless humility.

Father, I thank You for the lessons You have taught me through my difficult experiences, the cycles of life, and my Spiritual Classroom. In addition, You have shown me that healthy boundaries are essential, and that requiring participation is not a sign of a hardened heart, but a reflection of true love and wisdom. Help me to encourage others to invest in their own growth, to bring their efforts, ideas, or even their rough drafts, so that together we may perfect their Spiritual Tilling (Cultivation) Process. Let me be willing to help, to guide, and to share, but grant me discernment that I do not enable dependency, entitlement, or ungratefulness. May I pour into others as You Divinely Lead me, and may I receive from others in humility and grace.

Lord, I pray that You would remove from me any Spirit of taking, using, or undervaluing others. Replace it with the Spirit of Generosity, Encouragement, and Partnership. Teach me to find joy in giving, not only of my resources but also of my time, wisdom, and support. Let my labor be fruitful, as Your Word promises in Proverbs 14:23: *"In all labor there is profit, but idle chatter leads only to poverty."* May I be diligent in all I do, refusing to take shortcuts or to benefit from the work of others without due participation or acknowledgment.

My Heavenly Father, I ask for Your forgiveness for the times I have acted in ways that reflect *The Mark of Thievery*, whether knowingly or unknowingly. Cleanse my heart, renew my mind, and strengthen me by Your Spirit to walk in integrity. Help me to see the value in every person, to honor their contributions, and to celebrate their achievements. Give me the courage to address situations with grace and honesty when I feel used or unappreciated, and to set boundaries that honor You and myself.

Let my life be a TESTIMONY of Divine Transformation, moving from selfishness to selflessness, from taking to giving, from using to uplifting. May I always remember that true creativity and blessing flow when I labor diligently and share willingly, *As It Pleases You.* In Jesus' Name I pray, Amen.

PRAYER OVERRIDE 83

The Mark of Thwarted Perceptions

Heavenly Father, I come before You today in awe of Your Divine Wisdom and Mercy. Lord, I acknowledge that the greatest snares I face are often set not by others, but by the limitations I allow to take root in my own mind. I confess that there have been times when I have fallen under *The Mark of Thwarted Perceptions*, believing the lie that my life and actions are too small to make a difference. In these moments, I have let self-doubt, comparison, and fear build invisible walls around my potential. Forgive me for every time I have allowed these thoughts to block Your Predestined Purpose for my life.

Father, I recognize that there are those who merely wish and want, but do not move forward with faith or determination. I do not want to live half-heartedly, paralyzed by envy, pride, or the urge to compete against others. I want to be among those who rise up with intention and integrity, doing what pleases You, not what pleases the world. Purify my motives, Lord. When I have allowed comparison to poison my Spirit, when I have measured my worth against the accomplishments of others, I ask that You Supernaturally Heal and Divinely Restore my perspective.

Help me to understand that my true calling is not found in rivalry or outward achievement, but in embracing the mission You have set before me. Remind me that my contribution, no matter how small it may seem, is valuable in Your sight. Grant me the strength to press forward with purpose, passion, and perseverance, rejecting every voice of negativity and self-doubt. Let me become a doer, not just a dreamer or a talker, but one who acts with the confidence that comes from being rooted in Your love and truth.

Lord, I surrender my inner image to You. I know that what is within me matters far more than what is seen on the outside. Cleanse my heart from every form of materialism, comparison, and the Judgmental Spirit. Teach me to value character over possessions, and to pursue the Fruits of the Spirit more than any outward adornment. Let my inner life reflect Your light so that my actions and attitudes bring honor to Your Name.

Father, I ask that You reveal to me the roots of any unworthiness, indifference, or negative habits that have taken hold within my soul. Break every chain that holds me back from fulfilling my Divine Blueprint. Help me to examine my thoughts, motives, and actions with honesty and integrity. May I never allow my past wounds or failures to spoil my credibility, capabilities, or creativity. Instead, let Your Spirit guide me into self-awareness and lasting transformation.

When I am tempted to run someone else's race, redirect my focus to the unique path You have set for me. Guard my heart from envy and jealousy. Fill my mind with positive, fruitful thoughts, and never let me sabotage my right to be happy and whole in You. Remind me that true joy is not found in shallow laughter, but in a heart surrendered to You, as Your Word in Proverbs 14:12-13 reminds me.

I pray for the humility and courage to recognize my shortcomings and work on them for the long haul. Make me willing to learn, question, analyze, and change so that I may fulfill the Spiritual Mission You have given me. Help me to distinguish between my personal goals and my God-Given Calling, Talents, and Gifts. Bring me into full agreement with my Divine Destiny, and let me use what You have entrusted to me as a SHIELD and a BLESSING for others, never as a source of pride or self-importance.

Father, I surrender to the leading of the Spirit even when I do not fully understand what You are doing and why. I yield to Your Infallible Guidance, trusting that You are working in me and through me for Your Everlasting Glory. Give me the faith to decrease so that You may increase, and use my life in Earthen Vessel for Divine Restoration and Supernatural Impact. May I speak life, encouragement, and hope into my dry bones, so that others may rise to their own greatness with Your Unbiased Grace at the forefront.

Thank You for the privilege of being part of Your Divine Plan. With this privilege, please allow me to walk with confidence, humility, and boldness, always seeking to make a difference as You Divinely Empower me to do what I do. But more importantly, grant me the Divine Tools and Ammunition to do what You have Spiritually Sealed and Spiritually Predestined me to do while feeding Your precious sheep. May my legacy be one of faith, transformation, and Spirit-Led living. In Jesus' Name I pray, Amen.

PRAYER OVERRIDE 84

The Mark of Toxicity

Heavenly Father, I come before You in deep humility, seeking Your Divine Wisdom and guidance as I confront *The Mark of Toxicity* in my life. Lord, I confess that there have been times when I have tolerated, participated in, or even contributed to toxic relationships, environments, and patterns. Sometimes I have done so knowingly, at other times out of ignorance or fear. I acknowledge that true love, as You designed it, is not meant to harm, abuse, or weaken me. Rather, it is to nurture, protect, and help me become the best version of myself in You, *Spirit to Spirit*.

Father, open my eyes to the behaviors and attitudes that invite or sustain toxicity in my life. Teach me to recognize manipulation, persistent negativity, emotional blackmail, dishonesty, and all forms of subtle or overt harm. Help me to see when I am enabling toxicity in others or when I am being drawn to it out of unresolved wounds, low self-esteem, or the fear of being alone. Grant me the courage to address these patterns and to seek Your healing from within.

Lord, I remember the lesson of the Prodigal Son. Just as he came to himself in the mud, I acknowledge that I must come to myself in my own places of brokenness. I thank You for the assurance that my mud does not define me, and that no opinion, judgment, or rejection from others can diminish the power of Your Divine Love and my ability to rise again. Teach me to wash myself with Your Unfailing Truth, to believe in the purpose, lessons, and training hidden within my struggles, and to return to You with a Spirit of Humility, Repentance, and Renewal.

I reject the Spirit of Envy, Jealousy, Bitterness, Pride, and Self-Righteousness that can grow in the shadows of toxicity. Cleanse me of every secret sin or hidden wound that might invite such Spirits into my life. Let me forgive myself, wash myself, and return to my Spiritual Home, knowing that Your Heavenly Arms are wide-open, waiting to embrace me with Your

Abundant Grace and Heavenly Celebration. Remind me that my healing is not dependent on anyone else's approval or understanding, but on my willingness to ACCEPT Your INVITATION to be made whole, *As It Pleases You*.

Father, grant me discernment to recognize toxic people, places, or patterns, and the strength to separate myself from them when necessary. Help me to love without strings attached, to offer kindness without becoming entangled in drama, and to hold firm boundaries that protect my Spirit and my peace. Let me be an agent of transformation, not only for myself but also for those I encounter, offering hope, encouragement, and a pathway to healing.

Help me to embrace the power of Spiritual Purification and Renewal. May I never deny myself the right to be cleansed, restored, and made new by Your Spirit. Remind me that every circumstance, every trial, and even every bit of mud has the potential to be redeemed for my good in the LIGHT of Your Glory. Empower me to change my perceptions, to heal my wounds, and to cultivate a positive, Christ-Centered mindset rooted in Love, Joy, Peace, Patience, Kindness, Goodness, Faithfulness, Gentleness, and Self-Control.

Lord, let me never lose sight of my Divine Birthright or Blueprint. As Jesus healed with mud and compassion, so may I find healing in my own life, trusting that You can use anything and anyone for Your Divine Purpose, Mission, or to teach us a lesson. Let me walk in the fullness of Spirit-Led living, moving from simply surviving to truly thriving. Give me the wisdom to recognize when I cannot fix a situation, a person, or a place, and the humility to focus on fixing myself, building the nesting place for Divine Wisdom to come forth and to remain, *As It Pleases You*.

Thank You, Father, for the PROMISE that all things work together for my good as I love You and answer my Divine Calling. May my life become a TESTIMONY of deliverance from toxicity, a beacon of hope for others, and a reflection of Your Unfailing Love in a broken world. In Jesus' Name I pray, Amen.

PRAYER OVERRIDE 85

The Mark of Triangulation

Heavenly Father, I come before You with a heart longing for true and honest connection, seeking Your Divine Wisdom as I face *The Mark of Triangulation* in my life and relationships. Lord, I confess that too often I have found myself tangled in webs of miscommunication, confusion, and division that arise when a third party is brought into conflicts or conversations that require only Christlike Character and honest dialogue. I recognize that this pattern favors the adversary and hinders the unity You desire for Your people.

Father, I ask for Your forgiveness for the times I have allowed myself to pass the buck, to withhold direct communication, or to let others control the narrative of my life. Help me to take responsibility for my words, my actions, and my relationships. Grant me the courage to speak with clarity, love, and respect, refusing to allow manipulation or indirectness to take root in my heart or within my community.

Lord, I acknowledge that You alone are the true Mediator, as stated in Hebrews 12:24. Remind me that I do not need a triangle of confusion to resolve what honesty, humility, and the Fruits of the Spirit can handle. Show me how to Spiritually Till (Cultivate) the areas of my life that are overgrown with the thorns of division, gossip, or avoidance. Help me to do the work necessary for my own healing, so that no one else can take credit for what You have called me to cultivate within myself.

Reveal to me the places where I have allowed cycles of déjà vu to waste my time, and teach me to see with new eyes, to practice vuja dé, and to find the hidden roots of my issues. May my perceptions shift so that I can break free from cycles of confusion and take the steps needed to restore unity and peace.

Father, remind me daily of the gift of self-control. Help me to master my thoughts, my impulses, and my reactions, so that I do not contribute to chaos or division. Empower me to act with discipline, restraint, and integrity, aligning every decision with Your Divine Will and the guidance of the Spirit. Let me be mindful of the consequences of neglecting self-control and the way it can break down the walls of my own vineyard.

Lord, let Your love be the answer to every form of triangulation and division in my life. Help me to put on love, the bond of perfect unity, as Your Word commands. Grant me the grace to love others without reservation, to forgive quickly, and to seek reconciliation whenever possible. May the Spiritual Law of Unity guide my interactions, drawing me closer to others and to You.

Show me how to be the Loving One, to love one person at a time, to close the door on hatefulness, and to be a beacon of hope and acceptance in a fractured world. Help me to recognize my own shortcomings, to extend mercy to those who are unaware of their hurtful actions, and to stand firm against outright evil.

Lord, may my life reflect the beauty of true unity, honest communication, and Spirit-Led Love, *As It Pleases You*. Let me be an agent of peace, healing, and restoration, always seeking to build up rather than tear down. May I honor You with my words, my intentions, and my relationships, striving always for the ONENESS that comes from Your Spirit. In Jesus' Name I pray, Amen.

PRAYER OVERRIDE 86

The Mark of Unfaithfulness

Heavenly Father, I come before You with a heart open to Your truth, seeking Your Divine Guidance and Righteous Mercy as I consider *The Mark of Unfaithfulness* in my life. Lord, I confess that there have been moments when I have not been faithful to You, to myself, or to others. Sometimes, I have been swayed by the Spirit of Deception, convincing myself with small or large lies that erode the foundation of the faithfulness You desire for me. I recognize that faithfulness is not only an outward commitment but a matter of the Mind, Body, Soul, and Spirit, tested in all I do, say, and think.

Father, Your Word reminds me that confidence in an unfaithful person is like a bad tooth or a foot out of joint. You ask for truth in my inward parts and honesty in the hidden places of my psyche. Therefore, I ask for the courage to face myself with sincerity. Help me to acknowledge not only my faults but also my motives and desires, so that I may walk in true faithfulness and integrity before You. Let me never fake righteousness or pretend to be what I am not. Instead, bring me to a place where I am renewed in knowledge, according to the Image of Christ, putting off the old self and putting on the new.

Lord, I understand that my faithfulness is constantly tested and that my choices reflect either alignment with You or with the ways of the world. Grant me the humility to admit when I have failed, the obedience to follow Your Divine Path, and the discipline to turn away from unrighteousness. Let me place You first in everything, seeking the guidance of the Holy Spirit and TESTING every Spirit to discern what is good and PLEASING in Your sight.

I pray for the strength to till the ground of my heart, cultivating the Tree of Life within me. Help me to grow, maintain, and harvest the Fruits of the Spirit, de-weeding anything that could cause my life to become a tree of death. Let my words, thoughts, actions, and attitudes reflect righteousness, peace, and gentleness, producing good fruit that honors You and BLESSES others.

Father, keep me aware of the dangers of Spiritual Dualism, the constant tension between good and evil, right and wrong, light and darkness. Grant me wisdom to know the difference, so that I do not allow my psyche to lead me astray. Give me the courage to set boundaries, seek accountability, and document my progress as I strive for purity, honesty, and growth. Let me celebrate small victories and be patient with myself as I learn to be faithful in all things.

Lord, I ask that You would protect me from the influence of others who may seek to taint my fruits. Help me to avoid the snares of unfaithfulness, both in myself and in those I allow into my life. Teach me to seek relationships and communities that encourage my growth in You. Let me be quick to forgive, eager to reconcile, and always willing to bear my own load, giving account to You alone.

May the wisdom from above fill my heart, bringing peace, gentleness, mercy, and good fruits, without partiality or hypocrisy. Let me sow the fruit of righteousness in peace and strive to win souls with love and faithfulness. Lord, I desire to override *The Mark of Unfaithfulness*, to align my life with Your Predetermined Truth, and to reflect Your Unfailing Faithfulness to all the world.

Thank You for Your Supernatural Patience and Your continual invitation to return to You, *Spirit to Spirit*. I commit my heart, my mind, and my actions to the path of faithfulness, trusting that You will supply all I need to walk uprightly before You. In Jesus' Name I pray, Amen.

PRAYER OVERRIDE 87

The Mark of Unforgiveness

Heavenly Father, I come before You humbled and seeking the grace to release any hold that unforgiveness has had on my heart. Lord, I confess that there are times when I have struggled to forgive, whether the wounds are deep or the offenses seem small. I recognize that *The Mark of Unforgiveness* is not always obvious, but it is a secret hook the enemy uses to keep me tethered to pain, resentment, trauma, and bitterness. I acknowledge that holding onto grudges only prolongs my suffering, disrupts my relationships, and blocks the flow of Your Spirit within me.

Father, I ask You to reveal any hidden hooks of unforgiveness in my life. Show me where hatred, bitterness, rudeness, or anger have taken root, even in subtle ways. Your Word commands me to let all bitterness, wrath, anger, and evil speaking be put away from me, and to embrace kindness, tenderheartedness, and forgiveness, just as Christ forgave me. Lord, help me to walk in the Spirit of Forgiveness, not as a burden, but as a GIFT and a PATHWAY to redemption and renewal.

I thank You that forgiveness is a hidden power within me, a Spiritual Seal that keeps me moving forward in the Spirit of Excellence, no matter what others may say or do. Remind me that forgiving others is not just for their sake, but for my own healing, peace, and freedom. I receive Your Divine Promise that if I confess my sins, You are faithful and just to forgive me and cleanse me from all unrighteousness. Let this truth wash away every remnant of unforgiveness from my soul.

Lord, I surrender the need to see change in others as a condition for my forgiveness. I trust You to do the work in their lives and to handle every outcome. My responsibility is to maintain a pure heart, using the Fruits of the Spirit and Christlike Character in every interaction. I release anger, hate, grudges, and resentment into Your Heavenly Hands, refusing to let them weigh me down or draw me back into cycles of hurt.

Teach me the power of choosing forgiveness, even when it is hard. Remind me that the Law of Forgiveness is limitless, while unforgiveness sets boundaries and limits on my growth and Spiritual Development. Help me to overcome evil with good, to FEED and BLESS my enemies, trusting that in doing so, I heap coals of fire that PURIFY and RESTORE both them and me.

Father, I ask for the humility to step back into the Spiritual Classroom if needed, transforming any victim mentality into a victorious one. Let the Spirit of Gratitude and peace fill my heart, so that *The Mark of Unforgiveness* never takes hold. Make me a vessel of reconciliation, healing, and grace, always ready to let go and let God.

Thank You, Lord, for the GIFT of forgiveness and the freedom it brings. May my life reflect Your Unadulterated Mercy, and may I be known as one who forgives quickly, loves deeply, and trusts You completely. In Jesus' Name I pray, Amen.

PRAYER OVERRIDE 88

The Mark of Ungratefulness

Heavenly Father, I come before You with a heart that longs to be filled with gratitude, seeking to release any traces of ungratefulness that may have crept into my life. Lord, I confess that at times I have overlooked Your benefits, taken blessings for granted, or allowed my desires and frustrations to overshadow the abundant goodness You have poured into my existence. Forgive me for the times when I have complained rather than praised, focused on lack instead of abundance, and allowed *The Mark of Ungratefulness* to cloud my Spirit and sense of good judgment.

Father, awaken my dry bones to the benefits of obedience and the hidden WHYs behind every blessing. Remind me that gratitude is not just a feeling, but a conscious choice and a HOLY PRACTICE that transforms my mind, heart, and relationships. Help me to be mindful of my words, thoughts, and actions, so that I may set a guard over my mouth and cultivate a Spirit of Positivity and Thankfulness in every circumstance.

Lord, teach me to ask myself the right questions so that I may understand what I truly value and why. Guide me to seek the motives behind my motivations, so that I can respond to both my likes and dislikes with maturity and grace. Show me the power of thoughtful reflection, honest communication, and respectful interactions as I strive to express gratefulness in all my relationships.

I thank You for the opportunity to find comfort and value even when my expectations are shattered. Help me to create win-win situations out of disappointments by seeing Your hand at work, even in the midst of challenging circumstances. Let gratefulness become my foundation, empowering me to deflect negativity, offer empathy, and affirm the worth of others.

Father, I invite Your Spirit to fill me with kindness, empathy, and a deep sense of appreciation for every person, place, and season in my life. May I become a vessel of gratitude who disarms anger, heals hurts, and uplifts those around me. Let my gratefulness open my eyes to new blessings every day and keep *The Mark of Ungratefulness* far from my heart.

Lord, I thank You for Your Righteous Faithfulness, for every BENEFIT and BLESSING, and for the power to transform negativity into praise. May my life be marked by thankfulness, authenticity, and a Spirit that finds joy in every circumstance. In Jesus' Name I pray, Amen.

PRAYER OVERRIDE 89

The Mark of Unkindness

Heavenly Father, I come before You in humility, seeking the grace to uproot *The Mark of Unkindness* from my life. Lord, I acknowledge that kindness is often neglected because of fear, pride, or a desire to protect myself from being used or hurt. I confess that I have sometimes withheld kindness when it seemed unpopular, inconvenient, or risky, forgetting that Your Word calls me to be kind, tenderhearted, and forgiving, just as You have forgiven me in Christ.

Father, teach me to see kindness not as a weakness, but as a powerful action rooted in love. Help me to remember that every act of genuine kindness is an act of strength and humility that PLEASES You and brings me closer to You, *Spirit to Spirit*. Let me never be swayed by the world's standards of toughness, but instead embrace meekness, mercy, and compassion as the true riches of Your Kingdom.

Lord, I surrender my stress, defensiveness, and old patterns of reacting from a place of fear or pain. Help me to master my emotions, to turn off the negative flow of adrenaline and cortisol, and to choose the Fruits of the Spirit instead. Let my Mind, Body, Soul, and Spirit work in harmony, so I do not become dysfunctional, powerless, or Kingdomly Unusable.

Guide me to practice lovingkindness even when I do not feel appreciated or when I find myself in negative environments. Give me the wisdom to think before I speak or react, to extend empathy to those whose lives have not been touched by love or peace, and to be patient with those who are still in survival mode. Help me to glorify You by offering praise, ordering my conversation aright, and inviting You into every situation and response.

Father, I ask for discernment to know when a blessing is from You. Let my actions, decisions, and words align with Your Word and exhibit the Fruits of the Spirit. If I am unsure, remind me to offer praise, seek Your guidance, and wait for Your clear direction. Teach me to repent quickly, assume responsibility for my mistakes, and approach every lesson as an opportunity to grow in grace and humility.

Lord, keep my heart teachable, humble, and willing to share Your goodness with others. Let me love my enemies, do good, and lend without expecting anything in return, trusting that my reward is in Your hands. May Your Genuine Kindness flow through me, touching the lives of the unthankful and the lost, and opening doors to Kingdomly Wisdom, Treasures, and Secrets.

Thank You for Your Endless Mercy and for showing me the power of kindness. Let my life be a reflection of Your Everlasting Love, and may I walk in the Spirit of Gentleness and Supernatural Strength every day. In Jesus' Name I pray, Amen.

www.DrYBur.com

PRAYER OVERRIDE 90

The Mark of Unpreparedness

Heavenly Father, I come before You recognizing my need for Your Divine Wisdom and Guidance as I seek to overcome *The Mark of Unpreparedness* in my life. Lord, I confess that there have been times when I have felt overwhelmed or unsure about where to begin, and in those moments, I have allowed procrastination, avoidance, or fear to hold me back. I admit that true preparedness is not a constant state, but a journey that begins with a single step. Help me to embrace the process, even when it feels slow or uncertain, trusting that each small act of preparation brings me closer to my Predestined Purpose.

Father, awaken my Spirit to the principle of alertness. Teach me to be watchful in every area of my life. Show me the value of devoting time to building myself up in You, even if it is just one moment at a time. Remind me that the discipline of Spiritual Breaks, prayer, worship, meditation, and time in Your Word brings forth a new level of awareness, discernment, and readiness to face whatever may come.

Lord, I ask for the courage to confront the fears that block my creativity and progress. Break the cycle of negative thinking, self-doubt, and the fear of failure or judgment. Fill me with the confidence to bring forth the ideas You have planted within me, knowing that every good and perfect gift comes from You. Help me to mind map, journal, question, and develop my thoughts with diligence and patience, trusting that the right timing will reveal the Genius Ideas that will BLESS others and GLORIFY Your Name.

Grant me the humility to learn from others, to receive instructions, and to value the wisdom of preparation, *As It Pleases You*. Give me the perseverance to continue when I face obstacles, criticism, or setbacks. Let me remember that my battle scars are not symbols of defeat but reminders of Your faithfulness and the lessons You have taught me along the way. Strengthen my resolve to move in the Spirit of Excellence, even when I feel unqualified or rough around the edges.

Father, help me to embrace both the simplicity and the power of taking one step at a time. Let me never despise small beginnings, but celebrate each step of progress, knowing that You are building something beautiful in and through me. Fill my mind with progressive, faith-filled ideas, and teach me to use the Opposite Effect when I find myself blocked or discouraged. May I always seek Your Divine Timing above my own, trusting that when I prepare the way, You will honor my efforts and bring forth MY FRUIT in due season.

Lord, I thank You for Your Unwavering Patience with me, for the Divine Wisdom You so freely give, and for the privilege of learning from Your Spirit. Let my life be MARKED by readiness, resilience, and a willingness to be led by You into new and greater things for the Greater Good of all mankind. In Jesus' Name I pray, Amen.

PRAYER OVERRIDE 91

The Mark of Unrepentance

Heavenly Father, I come before You with a heart yearning for true transformation, seeking Your Divine Mercy and Supernatural Wisdom as I confront *The Mark of Unrepentance* in my life. Lord, I acknowledge that there have been times when I have hesitated to repent, fearing the exposure of my shortcomings, mistakes, or hidden struggles. I confess that I have sometimes allowed my psyche to rule, letting pride or avoidance keep me from the freedom that repentance brings. Yet, Your Word calls me to repentance, not as a punishment, but as an invitation to enter the Kingdom within me, to receive healing, renewal, and deeper fellowship with You.

Father, grant me understanding of what it means to repent. Reveal to me that repentance is not merely admitting fault, but is a profound state of metanoia (a change of mind, heart, and Spirit) that opens the door to new awareness and abundant life. Teach me to embrace the call to turn away from all that displeases You, and to make the meaningful adjustments that align my desires, actions, and thoughts with Your Divine Will. Let me recognize the areas where I need to change, and give me the courage to confess, to feel genuine remorse, and to seek the restoration that only You can provide.

Lord, I ask for the humility to take responsibility for my actions, to admit when I have hurt others, and to make amends where necessary. Allow me to face shame and guilt with honesty, knowing that You cover me with grace and that Your forgiveness is sure. Help me to reflect on the impact of my words, beliefs, and behaviors, and to allow Your Spirit to lead me in the process of true change for the Greater Good.

Father, let repentance pave the way for my healing, for restitution, and for the reconciliation of broken relationships. Give me the willingness to seek forgiveness from those I have wronged and to extend forgiveness to others, creating opportunities for restoration and mutual respect. Guard my Spirit from stubbornness or denial, and break every chain of pride or fear that would keep me from seeking You with a sincere and contrite heart.

Lord, remind me always that repentance is a GIFT, a pathway to renewal and abundant life. Let me never grow weary of coming before You with my failures and frailties, trusting that Your Righteous Mercy is new every morning. May my life be marked by continual transformation, as I surrender my will, my desires, and my ways to You, knowing that only in repentance can I find true freedom and peace.

Thank You, Father, for the power of repentance, for the grace to change, and for the promise of restoration. May I walk in *Spirit to Spirit* communion with You, never marked by unrepentance, but always open to Your loving correction and renewal at all times, and *As It Pleases You.* In Jesus' Name I pray, Amen.

PRAYER OVERRIDE 92

The Mark of Unrestraint

Heavenly Father, I come before You, recognizing the subtle ways *The Mark of Unrestraint* can take hold in my life. Lord, I acknowledge that in Your eyes, there is nothing normal about living without boundaries, even when the world tries to convince me otherwise. Your Word makes it clear that whoever has no rule over his own Spirit is like a city broken down, without walls. I confess that there have been times when I have cast off restraint, allowing impulses, desires, or emotions to guide my actions rather than the wisdom and discipline You have called me to embody.

Father, I ask for Your forgiveness for the moments when I have ignored the Law of Restraint, failing to pause, reflect, and act in alignment with Your Divine Will. Teach me to see restraint not as a limitation, but as a conscious choice that protects my Spirit, fortifies my character, and honors Your Divine Order. Help me to understand that the boundaries You set are not burdens, but blessings that safeguard my heart and keep me on the path of righteousness.

Lord, grant me the wisdom to exercise restraint in my thoughts, words, and actions, especially when faced with provocation or temptation. Let me be slow to anger, patient in adversity, and thoughtful in every decision. Strengthen my conscience as my Spiritual Compass, guiding me to recognize when I am off track, when pride or disobedience is present, or when I have overstepped my boundaries. Remind me to Spiritually Till (Cultivate) my own ground, to be about my Father's business, and to prioritize Your Divine Will above my own impulses.

Give me the courage to hold back when impulsiveness beckons, to seek understanding before passing judgment, and to choose justice, mercy, and humility in all my dealings. Help me to embrace the discipline of self-restraint, knowing that it builds trust, cultivates wisdom, and honors the greater good. Let the Fruits of the Spirit: Love, Joy, Peace, Patience,

Kindness, Goodness, Faithfulness, Gentleness, and Self-Control, be evident in every area of my life.

Father, may I never become numb to the dangers of unrestraint, nor allow it to become embedded in my character. Open my eyes to the consequences of my actions and grant me the strength to choose what is right, even when it is difficult. Let my life reflect the beauty of discipline and order, so that I may be a Divine Vessel of Your Abundant Peace, Justice, and Love in a world that desperately needs it.

Thank You for the gift of conscience, for the guidance of Your Spirit, and for the freedom that comes from living within Your Spiritual Boundaries. May I always be watchful, alert, and committed to Spiritual Growth, avoiding the chokehold of unrestraint while walking in the fullness of Your Divine Will. In Jesus' Name I pray, Amen.

PRAYER OVERRIDE 93

The Mark of Unsafety

Heavenly Father, I come before You aware of the reality of *The Mark of Unsafety*, both in the physical and Spiritual realms. Lord, I acknowledge that safety is not only a matter of external conditions, but also a matter of the heart, mind, and Spirit. I confess that there have been times when I have ignored the red flags, neglected Your sacred warnings, or failed to protect myself from unsafe environments and people. Forgive me for every moment of willful ignorance, denial, or self-deception that has drawn me into harm's way or left me vulnerable to the enemy's schemes.

Father, I thank You for the GIFT of my conscience. Lord, I need that sacred nudge or red flag from within that alerts me to danger, risk, or Spiritual Compromise. Teach me to recognize and honor those signals, never downplaying or disregarding the warnings You provide. Grant me wisdom and discernment to identify unsafe people, behaviors, and situations, whether they are overt or hidden in the guise of friendship, family, or opportunity. Let me not be deceived by controlling behaviors, persistent negativity, lack of respect, or any Spirit that seeks to exploit or endanger my well-being.

Lord, I ask for the courage to create and maintain boundaries that protect my Mind, Body, Soul, and Spirit. Fill me with vigilance, alertness, and a commitment to self-awareness, so that I am not caught off guard by the underhanded sifting that occurs when I am Spiritually Asleep. Remind me to pray upon awakening and before resting, covering my mind and dreams with Your Divine Presence and the Blood of Jesus. Help me to be prayed up, discerning, and always prepared for the enemy's tactics.

Father, when I face shattered expectations or any form of Spiritual Disappointments, teach me to trust in Your Divine Goodness and to guard my heart from bitterness or despair. Show me how to operate with the Fruits of the Spirit, to give thanks in all things, and to seek Your Divine Will above my own desires. Let me learn from my experiences, extract the win-win, and move on in faith, never returning to the places or patterns that You have delivered me from.

Lord, I ask that You would keep me in zones of protection, both physically and Spiritually. Surround me with Your Heavenly Angels, cover me with Your Divine Grace, and guide me by the Holy Spirit. May I never take safety for granted, but always honor it as a sacred responsibility for myself and those around me. Empower me to provide safe environments for others, to be a refuge of kindness, wisdom, and peace in a world that often feels unsafe.

Thank You for Your Abounding Faithfulness, and for the ways You alert, protect, and guide me. Let me walk in the fullness of Spiritual Excellence, never marked by unsafety, but always anchored in Your Divine Love, Presence, and Wisdom. In Jesus' Name I pray, Amen.

PRAYER OVERRIDE 94

The Mark of Urgency

Heavenly Father, I come before You recognizing the grip that *The Mark of Urgency* can have on my life. Lord, I confess that I have often been swept up in the rush of deadlines, pressure, and rapid decisions, sometimes neglecting to seek Your Divine Wisdom and peace before I act. I acknowledge that urgency, when unchecked, can cloud my judgment, open me to manipulation, and lead me down paths that do not honor You or Your purpose for me.

Father, I thank You for the gift of discernment and the power of pause. Remind me that not every urgent demand is truly urgent according to Kingdom Protocol, Principles, and Standards. Teach me to step back, breathe, and assess every situation with a clear mind and a calm Spirit. Let me not fall prey to high-pressure tactics or the temptation to react hastily, but instead grant me the courage to ask the right questions, to weigh the consequences, and to seek Your Divine Counsel above all else.

Lord, awaken me to the motivations that drive me. Help me to recognize what stirs my heart, whether it is the desire for success, praise, recognition, or love. Let me not be led astray by fleeting benefits or the appearance of urgency, but ground me in the truth of Your Word. Revive my dry bones, O Lord, and quicken my Spirit according to Your Righteous Judgments and Enduring Mercies.

In addition, O Lord, give me the wisdom to discern real deadlines from artificial ones, and the strength to resist manipulation from any source. Fill me with peace in the midst of pressure, and teach me that my value is not found in how quickly I can respond, but in how faithfully I seek Your Divine Will. Let my actions be marked by careful consideration, patience, and a deep trust in Your Divine Timing while operating *As It Pleases You*.

Father, I ask that You protect me from the pitfalls of hasty decisions, oversight, and regret. Let every choice I make reflect Your Divine Wisdom, bringing glory to Your Name and BLESSINGS to those around me. May I become a person who motivates others not by urgency, but by gentleness, awareness, and Spirit-Led discernment.

Thank You for Your tender mercies and for reviving me according to Your Word. May I walk confidently, unhurried and anchored in Your Heavenly Presence, always ready to hear Your Sacred Voice above the noise. In Jesus' Name I pray, Amen.

PRAYER OVERRIDE 95

The Mark of Victimization

Heavenly Father, I come before You with a heart seeking freedom from *The Mark of Victimization*, whether I have carried it as a silent burden or perpetuated it in my words, actions, thoughts, beliefs, biases, or attitudes. Lord, I acknowledge that victimization is not always visible on the outside but can shape the way I see myself, others, and even You. I confess that there have been times when I have allowed my wounds, traumas, injustices, fears, false expectations, or the pain of my past to define me, leaving me stuck in a cycle of helplessness, resentment, or separation from Your Divine Purpose and Presence.

Father, I ask for the courage and humility to recognize not only where I have been a victim, but also where I may have contributed to the victimization of others, intentionally or unintentionally, through my words, judgments, biases, or actions. Cleanse me of any tendency to judge, control, or exclude, and fill me with compassion, empathy, and the desire to restore others as You have restored me.

Lord, I thank You for the example of Jesus who healed the man with the withered hand in Mark 3:1-6, teaching us that there is no wrong time to do good and that restoration is always within reach. Help me to stretch out my hand in faith, to receive healing for my own hidden withering, and to extend GRACE and BLESSINGS to others who are suffering. May I never overlook the weak places in my own life or the lives of those around me, but instead speak life, hope, and encouragement wherever I go.

Father, when storms arise, and I feel tossed about by the issues of life, remind me to activate my faith, cast down fear, and rebuke every force that seeks to keep me bound. Teach me to put on the Whole Armor of God, to stand firm against principalities and powers, and to fight back with prayer, fasting, and the Spiritual Authority You have given me. As a Child of the Most High God, let my WORDS and ACTIONS be guided by the Fruits of the Spirit, knowing there is no law against Love, Joy, Peace, Patience, Kindness, Goodness, Faithfulness, Gentleness, and Self-Control.

Lord, help me to accept the help and healing You send, even when it comes in unexpected ways. Give me Spiritual Discernment to recognize true deliverance, the Supernatural Wisdom to guard my TESTIMONY, and the humility to move forward without returning to former habits or places of defeat or vomit. Teach me to walk in worthiness, not defined by others' acceptance or rejection, but by the truth of who You created me to be.

Father, I pray for the strength to stand in the gap for others, especially for children and those unable to fight their own battles. Let me be a Divine Vessel of Restoration, Hope, and Protection, using my experiences to bring HEALING rather than perpetuate harm.

Thank You for the miracles You have worked in my life, for every moment of restoration, and for the call to rise up and walk in the fullness of my Blueprinted Purpose. May I never again be marked by victimization, but instead walk in Supernatural Victory, Abounding Faith, and Spirit-Led Lovingkindness, BLESSING others as I have been BLESSED. In Jesus' Name I pray, Amen.

Dr. Y. Bur

www.DrYBur.com

PRAYER OVERRIDE 96

The Mark of Weakness

Heavenly Father, I come before You acknowledging every place in my life where *The Mark of Weakness* has tried to define me. Lord, I confess that hopelessness, disappointment, and the noise of other people's agendas have sometimes overshadowed my sense of purpose. I have relived my past mistakes, searched for wholeness in all the wrong places, and allowed the world's standards and fleeting trends to shape my identity. Forgive me for the times I have lost sight of who You created me to be, for comparing myself to others, and for living for approval that does not satisfy my soul.

Father, I recognize that my ego and pride can only be subdued by humility. I surrender my Competitive Spirit and my desire to emulate others, choosing instead the guidance of the Holy Spirit and the Fruits of the Spirit as my Navigational Tools. Teach me to walk in Love, Joy, Peace, Patience, Kindness, Goodness, Faithfulness, Gentleness, and Self-Control. May these qualities shine in my actions, habits, and desires, restoring my hope and confidence in You, *Spirit to Spirit*.

Lord, I ask You to help me pick up the pieces of my life with Spiritual Awareness. Show me the root causes or seeds behind my fears, guilt, anger, and negative emotions. Let me learn from my past, so I do not carry unnecessary baggage into my future. Even as I acknowledge the reality of bondage, I trust in Your Supernatural Power to deliver and equip me. Grant me the discernment to see the seeds of deception and the courage to seek truth, ask questions, and walk in righteousness, clothed with Your Divine Truth and Your Breastplate of Righteousness.

Father, mold my heart and mind to be PLEASING in Your sight, unaffected by the opinions or feelings of man. Guard me against bitterness, division, and the traps of the enemy that seek to keep me from my inheritance. Fill me with forgiveness for myself and others, knowing that Your Divine Mercy is more than enough to cover my shortcomings and theirs. Let me be quick to give burdens over to You, never allowing resentment or unforgiveness to hold me captive.

Lord, I place myself in Your Spiritual Classroom, eager to learn, grow, and transition as You see fit. Build and prune my character, sharpen my people skills, and lead me from old to new. Show me how to cancel the journey into despair and call upon the Holy Trinity for strength and restoration. I renounce the flow of selfish idolatry and embrace my authority as Your child, equipped and empowered to overcome every PIT that life may present.

Thank You for the reservoir of hope, strength, and wisdom that is mine through Christ. May I walk daily in Spirit-Led Confidence, knowing that my worth is found in You alone. Let my life be a TESTIMONY of Your Divine Power to turn weakness into strength, despair into joy, and defeat into victory. In Jesus' Name I pray, Amen.

www.DrYBur.com

PRAYER OVERRIDE 97

The Mark of Wickedness

Heavenly Father, I come before You in awe of Your Unwavering Holiness and Enduring Mercy, seeking Your truth as I confront *The Mark of Wickedness* in my life. Lord, I confess that wickedness is not just an image from a story but a real force that can take root in my heart, mind, thoughts, words, and actions if I do not remain vigilant. I recognize that wickedness is not merely breaking rules or outward appearances, but a departure from Your Divine Will, a straying from Your Divine Righteousness, Justice, and Love.

Father, search my heart and mind. Reveal to me any waywardness, rebellion, stubbornness, or idolatry that has crept in, even unawares. I pray as David did: Search me, O God, and know my heart; try me, and know my anxieties; see if there is any wicked way in me, and lead me in the way everlasting. Only You know the deepest motives and intentions that lie within. Cleanse me of everything that stands in opposition to Your Spirit and Your Divine Ways or Word.

Lord, grant me the humility to accept Your correction and the grace to repent quickly and sincerely. Teach me to recognize how my choices, thoughts, and alliances either honor or grieve You. Keep me from the traps of disobedience, rebellion, and stubbornness. Break every soul tie that I have to any form of idols, whether they be people, platforms, pride, or secret desires. Remind me that there are no shortcuts in Your Kingdom, and Your judgment is just and true.

Father, I ask for a heart that is trustworthy and a Spirit that can be entrusted with Your Divine Wisdom, Knowledge, and Understanding. Guard me from ever using my Divine Gifts to harm, expose, or belittle others. Let me be a Divine Vessel of Redemption, Compassion, and Grace, always seeking reconciliation and never division. May I honor the privacy and dignity of others, using my words for encouragement and truth, never for gossip or harm.

Lord, deliver me from confusion and worthlessness. Align my heart, mind, and Spirit with Your Divine Nature, so that I walk in Divine Holiness, Humility, and Love. Help me to discern when my motives are slipping, and quickly return to You in repentance. Teach me to handle Kingdom secrets with reverence, never abusing the trust You extend.

Thank You for the Power of the Blood of Jesus, which cleanses, redeems, and restores me when I come with a repentant heart. May I live daily in awe of Your Divine Grace, never taking it for granted or using it as a license to sin. Let my life be marked by trustworthiness, righteousness, and a desire to GLORIFY You in all things. In Jesus' Name I pray, Amen.

PRAYER OVERRIDE 98

The Mark of Worthlessness

Heavenly Father, I come before You with a heart longing to be free from *The Mark of Worthlessness*, which has silently gripped so many in this generation, including myself. Lord, I confess that I have sometimes measured my worth by appearances, achievements, or the fleeting approval of others, instead of seeing myself through Your loving eyes. I admit that I have hidden feelings of inadequacy, insecurity, and disappointment behind a mask of confidence, success, or indifference. Too often, I have allowed comparison and self-judgment to shape my actions, thoughts, and relationships.

Father, I acknowledge the power of unresolved pain, negative self-talk, and unmet expectations to sow seeds of worthlessness within me. Yet, I thank You for the HEALING GIFT of Compassion. Teach me to approach myself and others with gentleness, understanding, and forgiveness. Let compassion become the bridge that heals my brokenness, interrupts cycles of pain, and transforms my story into a TESTIMONY of HOPE.

Lord, help me to recognize that every person, including myself, carries wounds, some visible, some hidden, and some unknown. May I never transfer my pain to others or allow my disappointments to cloud my judgment or kindness. Instead, fill me with the Spirit of Excellence, that I might choose patience, understanding, and genuine love, even in the midst of frustration or fear. Show me how to listen actively, offer encouragement, and validate the feelings of others, while also embracing my own humanity with honesty and grace.

Father, I pray for the courage to confront my struggles openly before You, allowing Your truth to dismantle every lie of worthlessness spoken over me or birthed within me. Let me find my value, not in the shifting sands of public opinion or worldly success, but in the unshakable foundation of Your Unfailing Love and Predestined Purpose for my life. Guard my heart from the Spirit of Comparison, the hunger for likes or validation, and the temptation to judge others based on outward appearances.

Lord, I ask that You would make compassion my guiding principle. Empower me to extend it to others as freely as You have extended it to me. Let my life become a safe haven for the hurting, a place where brokenness is met with understanding and hope. May compassion rain down on the droughts of my soul and those around me, breaking the yoke of brokenness and releasing new cycles of healing, growth, and joy.

Thank You for the PROMISE that when I choose compassion, I invite Your Spirit to move freely in and through my life. May I walk daily in the fullness of my God-Given Worth, uplifting those around me, and glorifying You in all that I do, say, and become for the Greater Good. In Jesus' Name I pray, Amen.

PRAYER OVERRIDE 99

The Mark of the X-Factor

Heavenly Father, I come before You today with a heart humbled by awe and gratitude for the mysteries You have woven into my being. I acknowledge that within me lies the X-Factor, that unique spark of unpredictability, the secret ingredient You have instilled to set me apart in Your Divine Design. I confess that at times, this X-Factor has been a source of both wonder and struggle. Sometimes it tempts me to act out of unpredictability, to lead with intentions, behaviors, and thoughts that are not anchored in Your Divine Will. Yet, I know that what You have placed within me is meant for good, not for disaster.

Lord, I seek Your Divine Wisdom to discern the depths of my X-Factor, to explore its four corners, and to starve the impulses that do not align with Your Divine Purpose for my life. Help me to understand the gifts, qualities, or characteristics that make me unique in You, *Spirit to Spirit*, not so I may glorify myself, but so I may glorify You in all that I do. May I never allow *The Mark of the X-Factor* to deprive me of what You have already ordained for me. Grant me the courage to stand out, *As It Pleases You*, and to walk faithfully in the calling You have placed upon my life.

Father, I recognize the dangers of cancel culture, the enemy's attempt to get me to self-cancel my hopes, dreams, desires, and purpose. I rebuke every scheme that seeks to render me hopeless, dreamless, desireless, or purposeless. I declare that I will not settle for whatever comes my way, nor will I fall for deception or distraction. Thus, I will not self-abort my Divine Mission.

Father, I cannot do this alone. My battle scars remind me of my total dependence on You. I lean on the Holy Trinity (Father, Son, and Holy Spirit) to feed my soul and prepare me to feed Your sheep. I renounce every excuse and recommit to preparing myself and others to receive the Divine Wisdom You have imparted throughout my Spiritual Journey.

Lord, I recognize that not all success is equal in You, according to Kingdom Principles and Standards. Blessings that come by effort, perseverance, and obedience carry a value far greater than those handed to me without struggle. Ignite in me a passion that is rooted in gratefulness, respect, and a selfless devotion to You, *Spirit to Spirit*.

My Heavenly Father, rid me of ungratefulness, selfishness, and any Spirit that operates apart from You. In addition, I ask that You cleanse me of every character flaw that threatens to X-Out my X-Factor:

- ☐ Remove from me an argumentative or chaotic Spirit.
- ☐ Deliver me from a deceptive or debaucherous Spirit.
- ☐ Free me from arrogance, greed, or a quick-tempered, uncontrollable Spirit.
- ☐ Break the chains of selfishness, anger, stinginess, competitiveness, or bullying.
- ☐ Purge from me the Spirit of Perfectionism, including superfluous righteousness, ungratefulness, nitpicking, victimization, negativity, stubbornness, disobedience, rebellion, coveting, envy, jealousy, overzealous pride, division, sabotage, unforgiveness, and unrepentantness.

I confess that my flaws can disconnect me from the fullness of Your Real Blessings and distort the fruits on my Tree of Life. Thus, I embrace the GIFTS of prayer, repentance, forgiveness, and fasting as DIVINE MEANS to keep my Spirit pure and my Predestined Purpose clear.

From this moment forward, I surrender my will to You, choosing willingness, obedience, and agreement over resistance. I ask for Your training, preparation, and equipping, knowing that You will withhold what I am not ready to receive for my protection. Teach me to control my words, thoughts, beliefs, desires, and actions so that I may be ready for the Divine Call.

Thank You for the privilege of carrying the X-Factor, for the honor of being called, and for the endless grace You extend as I grow in Spiritual Authority and Maturity. Mold me, use me, and keep me ever mindful that all I have and all I am is for Your Everlasting Glory. In Jesus' Name I pray, Amen.

PRAYER OVERRIDE 100

The Mark of Yoking

Heavenly Father, I come before You with a heart open to Your Heavenly Truths, seeking Your Divine Presence as I reflect on *The Mark of Yoking*. Lord, I recognize that the power You have placed within me is both a blessing and a burden, and I confess that my natural inclination is to choose the blessing and flee from anything that binds me. Yet, I understand that when it comes to my Divine Destiny, You do not make the path easy. The enemy tries to block my progress, but You use every resistance as both my PROTECTION and Spiritual Training.

Father, I ask You to enlighten me about the marks that link my soul to others. I know that *The Mark of Yoking* can become the very thing that either liberates or imprisons me. If I lack preparation, *As It Pleases You*, I risk being broken down to the core. Grant me wisdom to discern every yoke and its influence in my life. My Lord, do not let me be deceived by superficial covers of pretense, for a yoke rarely appears as a yoke. For this reason, I fully understand that a yoke may come as an obligation, a relationship, a burden, or a connection that binds, unites, or constrains. Therefore, I ask for equal yokes, not unequal ones, for it is inequality that weighs down my Spirit and mind.

Lord, I refuse to settle for mediocrity or accept mere scraps from life. I choose to speak life to my dry bones and to RISE in the POWER of Your Spirit. Let me never abandon the journey that began in the Spirit to finish in the flesh. Let me walk in the Spirit of Excellence and operate in good character, always remaining on the side of what is good, right, and positive.

Heavenly Father, I reject the Spirit of Defeat and Poverty. I will not walk in shame or disbelief, for You are the same yesterday, today, and forevermore. I will not speak as one who is forsaken, but as one who is BLESSED by Your Heavenly Hand. Help me to stand with confidence in the Promises of Heaven, living as a true child of the King.

Lord, where Your people are divided, unfocused, prideful, or biased, I pray that You would realign our hearts. Remove the Spirit of Hatred, Competition, and Jealousy from among us. Let us not drag one another through the dirt, but instead lift one another up in love and unity. I ask that You awaken the Body of Christ to our Spiritual Rights and the GREATNESS of the GIFTS You have invested in each of us. Our backgrounds, skills, perspectives, and Spiritual Gifts are designed to be our GREATEST STRENGTH, not a source of division. Help us to collectively pull the WEALTH of the Kingdom out of the pews and into action, cultivating every seed You have planted.

Father, I ask You to break every yoke in my life that has been formed by ignorance, pride, or the influence of those who have misused Your Spiritual Laws. Where I have allowed others to turn Your Kingdom Principles against me, I ask You to RESTORE my understanding and make me better, stronger, and wiser, *As It Pleases You*. I recognize that You show no partiality, and Your rain falls on the righteous and unrighteous alike. Help me to sow righteousness so that I may have a sure REWARD in Earthen Vessel for my Heaven on Earth Experiences.

Search my heart and reveal to me any self-induced yokes, whether through my character, my thoughts, my words, or my actions. Teach me the ways of Spiritual Duality, Divine Dominion, and Spiritual Fruits. Free me from the lust of the eyes, the lust of the flesh, and the pride of life. Help me to recognize every yoke for what it is, without rationalizing or justifying it. Whatever keeps me from being one with You, one with myself, or one with others, I surrender it now and ask You to break it, in the Name of Jesus.

Lord, open my Spiritual Eye so that my whole body is full of light. Let me see as You see and not be blinded by my earthly vision. Give me discernment to recognize the difference between what is counterfeit and what is Divinely Ordained. Help me to remove the plank from my own eye before I consider the speck in my brother's eye. Let my mind's eye become one with Your Eye so that I may walk in Spiritual Empowerment and Clarity.

Unite me with You, with myself, and with others, *As It Pleases You*. Remove every mark of division, every trace of zombie-like existence, and restore my soul to the path of righteousness. Help me to master Your Spiritual Laws so I may override every mark of the enemy and walk boldly in my Divine Purpose. Thank You, Lord, for Your unfailing love, Your enduring PROMISES, and the POWER of Your Spirit to break every yoke. In Jesus' Name I pray, Amen.

PRAYER OVERRIDE 101

The Mark of Zombieism

Heavenly Father, I come before You with a humble heart, recognizing my need for Your Divine Wisdom, guidance, and the presence of Your Holy Spirit. Lord, I confess that there are times when my thoughts and actions become so automated, so void of intention and connection, that I feel as though I am walking dead while still alive. I have seen myself and others moving through life as if in a trance, perceiving each other only as shadows or trees, not as the beloved souls You have created. When my Mind, Body, Soul, and Spirit are asleep, I find myself merely going through the motions, disengaged from the fullness of the life You have promised.

Father, I ask You to awaken every part of my being. Breathe new life into my dry bones, just as You did for the valley of dry bones in Ezekiel, because I refuse to accept *The Mark of Zombieism*. Instead, I choose to speak life, hope, and joy into my existence. Your Word says in Proverbs 17:22, *"A joyful heart is good medicine, but a crushed spirit dries up the bones."* Lord, fill my heart with Your joy and heal every place where my Spirit has been wounded or crushed.

I pray for people, places, and things that are under the weight of Spiritual Slumber and Lifelessness. I ask that You would protect me and those I love from any who would prey upon our weaknesses, naivety, or innocence. Deliver us from the vultures that seek to exploit, oppress, or devour. Expose any patterns of behavior in me that contribute to cycles of abuse, including Mental, Physical, Emotional, or Spiritual, and grant me the courage to break them in Your Name.

Father, for those who have not learned how to usher in Your Spirit, grant us the grace to offer sacrifices of praise, thanksgiving, repentance, and the reading of Your Word. I plead the Blood of Jesus over my life, my family, my community, and all that concerns me. Cleanse and purify me, Lord. Let no Unholy Spirit find a place in my life, for I stand COVERED by the Blood of the Lamb.

Remind me that Spiritual Laws remain, what I sow, I will reap. Let the seeds I plant be seeds of love, compassion, kindness, humility, gentleness, and patience, as Colossians 3:12 instructs. Where I lack compassion, reveal my love deficit, and heal it by the power of Your Spirit. Let Your Untainted Love be the glue that bonds me to You, to myself, and to others. Fill me up again and again, O Lord, until I overflow in Your Divine Fruits.

Teach me to love my enemies, to bless those who curse me, to do good to those who hate me, and to pray for those who spitefully use me and persecute me. Help me to remember that You make Your sun to rise on the evil and the good, and send rain on the just and the unjust. Guard my heart against judgment and self-righteousness. Let compassion and understanding be my guide, so that I extend to others the same mercy I hope to receive.

Strengthen me so that I am always standing on the Rock, Christ Jesus, and not on my own understanding. Remind me that restoration follows rejection, and that Your Divine Purpose is always at work, even in my pain or confusion.

Help me to speak words that heal and unite, not words that wound or divide. Let my people skills and the Fruits of the Spirit be the true evidence of my relationship with You. Guard my tongue, so that I do not lead anyone astray by my words or actions. Let patience, kindness, self-control, and gentleness be the hallmarks of my speech and conduct.

Your truth has set me free. Your statutes rejoice my heart and enlighten my eyes. I will look for the good, the positive, and the fruitful in every situation. Let Your Word be a lamp to my feet and a light to my path.

From this moment forward, I speak life into my dry bones, knowing that You, Lord, are faithful to complete the good work You have begun in me. Restore what has been lost, release what has held me down, heal what has been wounded, and replace betrayal with true companionship. I lift my head and step into my future with boldness, because You are with me. I own my victory, for You have already won it for me at the Cross.

Thank You, Lord, for the ammunition of the Fruits of the Spirit. Thank You for the Spiritual Gifts, the Divine Calling, and the Creative Talents You have placed within me. I choose to use them to BLESS others and bring GLORY to Your Name. In Jesus' Name I pray, Amen.

www.ingramcontent.com/pod-product-compliance
Lightning Source LLC
Chambersburg PA
CBHW050243170426
43202CB00015B/2898